Editor
Eric Migliaccio

Editor in Chief
Karen J. Goldfluss, M.S. Ed.

Creative Director
Sarah M. Fournier

Cover Artist
Barb Lorseyedi
Marilyn Goldberg

Illustrator
Donna Bizjak

Art Coordinator
Renée Mc Elwee

Imaging
James Edward Grace
Craig Gunnell

Publisher
Mary D. Smith, M.S. Ed.

Rigorous READING

In-Depth Guide

TCR 8260

M000100136

HOLES
Louis Sachar

Teacher Created Resources

Author
Karen McRae

CORRELATED TO COMMON CORE STANDARDS

For correlations to the Common Core State Standards, see pages 79–80 of this book or visit *http://www.teachercreated.com/standards.*

Teacher Created Resources
12621 Western Avenue
Garden Grove, CA 92841
www.teachercreated.com

ISBN: 978-1-4206-8260-1

© 2016 Teacher Created Resources
Made in U.S.A.

Teacher Created Resources

TABLE OF CONTENTS

Introduction 3

How to Use This Book 4

    A Custom Resource — Keeping Novel Logs — Complete Lesson Plan

Novel Information 7

    Book Summary — About the Author — Make It a Text Set!

Pre-Reading Activities 8

    Judging a Book — "C" Where You Stand

Interactive Novel Logs 10

    What Happened When? — A Dynamic Protagonist — Major Minors — All Types of
    Trouble — Choice Words — Crystal Ball

Sections from *Holes*

Section I: Chapters 1–7 16

    Teacher Instructions — *Individual:* "The Parts of *Holes*" — *Individual:* "Setting the
    Mood" — *Collaborative:* "Tone vs. Mood" — *Individual:* "Then and Now" —
    Individual: "Section I Log-In"

Section II: Chapters 8–19 22

    Teacher Instructions — *Collaborative:* "A Long Look at Lizards" — *Individual:* "The
    Boys of Group D" — *Individual:* "Zero In" — *Individual:* "Section II Log-In"

Section III: Chapters 20–28 28

    Teacher Instructions — *Individual:* "Chain of Events" — *Collaborative:* "Speaking of
    the Warden" — *Individual:* "What It Really Means" — *Individual:* "The Onion Man" —
    Individual: "The Antagonists" — *Individual:* "Section III Log-In"

Section IV: Chapters 29–32 35

    Teacher Instructions — *Individual:* "All Kinds of Unkind" — *Individual:* "The New Kid"
    — *Individual:* "Left in Suspense" — *Individual:* "Section IV Log-In"

Section V: Chapters 33–42 41

    Teacher Instructions — *Individual:* "Desert Decisions" — *Collaborative:* "Scavenger
    Hunt" — *Individual:* "A Tale of Two" — *Individual:* "A Change in Stanley" —
    Individual: "Section V Log-In"

Section VI: Chapters 43–50 47

    Teacher Instructions — *Individual:* "The Return to Camp" — *Individual:* "While They
    Were Gone" — *Collaborative:* "Layer by Layer" — *Individual:* "The Final Chapter" —
    Individual: "Same Old Song?" — *Individual:* "Section VI Log-In"

TABLE OF CONTENTS (CONT.)

Post-Reading Activities 54

Teacher Instructions — *Individual:* "Add It Up" — *Individual:* "A Better Letter?" — *Collaborative:* "An Honest Ad?" — *Individual:* "A New Point of View" — *Individual:* "Considering Genre" — *Individual:* "Filling In the Holes" — *Collaborative:* "A Character Interview" — *Collaborative:* "A Novel Poster" — *Collaborative:* "Connect the Plots" — *Individual:* "Family Fortune" (Outline — Self-Editing Checklist — Peer-Editing Checklist) — *Individual:* "A Persuasive Letter" — *Individual:* "My Book Rating"

Words to Know 74

Teacher Instructions — Novel Vocabulary

Answer Key 76

Meeting Standards 79

+ +

INTRODUCTION

Read through the Common Core Standards for "Reading: Literature," and you will find that the work expected of students is expressed using such academic terminology as *describe*, *determine*, *develop*, *support*, and *cite*. Requirements such as these cannot be met via the comprehension-question worksheets and culminating quizzes that have long been the staples of literature guides designed for classroom use. The primary objective of those traditional activities was to make sure that students were keeping track of what was happening in the section of the novel that they had just read. Very little rigor and synthesis was asked of students, and usually none until the entire novel was read.

From a teacher's standpoint, this style of classroom analysis misses multiple opportunities to delve deeply into the details that make a specific piece of literature a classic; from a student's standpoint, this way to reflect on literature is monotonous and inflexible, and it fails to nurture the momentum experienced when one is invested in a compelling work of art. That is why the guides in the *Rigorous Reading* series aim to do much more: they aim to transform the reading of a great novel into a journey of discovery for students.

Instead of merely asking students what happened in any given section, this resource asks questions that require closer reading and deeper analysis—questions such as "Why did the author choose to include this information?" and "How does this information further the plot or offer more insight into the themes, characters, settings, etc.?" And instead of waiting until the end of the novel to put the pieces of the puzzle in place, students will learn to add to and alter their understanding of the novel *as they are reading it*. The various activities in this resource systematically prompt students to consider and appreciate the many ingredients the author has combined to form the novel as a whole.

A CUSTOM RESOURCE

This in-depth guide has been written specifically for Louis Sachar's *Holes*. The lessons and activities have been structured and scaffolded to maximize the experience of reading and teaching this novel.

To prepare your students for their reading of *Holes*, utilize the **novel information** and **pre-reading activities** included on pages 7–9 of this guide. Included in this section is information about the book and its author, along with activities designed to acclimate students to the themes and/or concepts present in the book they are about to read.

This resource provides activities that help foster comprehension and reinforce knowledge of literary elements as students read *Holes*. These **section activities** allow students the opportunity to process short sections of the novel at a time, laying a strong foundation for their ability to engage more deeply with the chapters to come. For each section of the novel, students will complete individual and collaborative activities that encourage close reading, referencing textual evidence, and drawing their own conclusions about the text.

Additionally, this resource provides students with another avenue through which they can reflect on recurring literary elements while also connecting personally with the novel. Each student maintains his or her own **Interactive Novel Log**, using it as a way to consider and then reconsider various aspects of the novel.

Upon completion of the entire novel, students can synthesize their ideas about the novel by completing several individual and/or collaborative **post-reading activities** on pages 54–73. This section of the resource contains larger assignments including group projects and essay assignments.

On pages 74–75, **vocabulary** lists are provided for each section of the novel, along with suggestions for ways to teach vocabulary during reading and after completing the novel.

At the end of this guide, an **answer key** is provided for activities that require specific answers, and a list identifies how each activity correlates to **Common Core State Standards**.

Key Notes

For a description of Interactive Novel Logs and how to use them in your classroom, see page 5 of this guide.

An ideal way to use this resource would be to follow the complete lesson plan given on page 6 of this guide.

The use of multiple texts can help build and extend knowledge about a theme or topic. It can also illustrate the similarities and differences in how multiple authors approach similar content or how an individual author approaches multiple novels. See the bottom of page 7 for suggestions about using *Holes* as part of a text set.

When teaching other novels in your classroom, consider using the specific ideas and also the general approach presented in this resource. Ask students to mine small sections of a novel for clues to theme and characterization. Examine the craft, structure, and purpose of select passages. Explore inferences and encourage connections.

This guide is designed for use in grades 5–8, and the standards correlations on pages 79–80 reflect this range. This leveling has been determined through the consideration of various educational metrics. However, teacher discretion should be used to determine if the novel and guide are appropriate for lower or higher grades, as well.

4

KEEPING NOVEL LOGS

Great works of literature are complex texts, and complex texts are multilayered. They enrich and reveal as they go along. Successful readers are those who "go along" with the novel, too. Interactive Novel Logs give students a place and a space to record their thoughts and observations as they journey through the book. After each section of the novel is read, students use their Interactive Novel Logs to track the introduction and development of such literary elements as plot, setting, theme, characterization, craft, and structure, while also choosing their own ways to connect the novel to their own life experiences.

Materials needed for each student:

✦ a three-ring binder or presentation folder

✦ a blank sheet of plain paper with holes punched for title page

✦ two or three sheets of blank lined paper for Table of Contents

✦ several extra sheets of paper (both lined and plain) for student's responses to the "Ideas for Your Interactive Log" prompts at the end of each section

> ### Key Notes
>
> One Interactive Novel Log can be kept for multiple novels, in which case a larger three-ring binder will be needed. If it will be used only for the activities included in this guide for *Holes*, a ½-inch binder or presentation folder will be adequate.

Assembling the Interactive Novel Log:

1. On the plain paper, allow students to design their own title page. Have them write "Interactive Novel Log" and *Holes* in the middle of the page. They should include their name and grade at the bottom. Allow students to decorate the page.

2. Add blank lined paper for the Table of Contents. Have students write "Table of Contents" at the top. They will add to this list as they create new pages.

3. Before reading each section of the novel, photocopy and distribute new copies of the Interactive Novel Log worksheets (pages 10–15). Directions for completing these activities can be found in the "Teacher Instructions" that begin Section I.

4. For the final activity in each section, photocopy and distribute the "Section Log-In" page for the section. Follow the directions given. Students select one or more of the four topics in the "Ideas for Your Interactive Log" section and create an Interactive Novel Log page that responds to that topic.

5. After the class has completed the entire novel and the post-reading activities, you may have students include the "My Book Rating" worksheet (page 73) as a final entry in their Interactive Novel Logs.

COMPLETE LESSON PLAN

The following lesson plan presents a systematic way to use this entire guide in your classroom study of *Holes* by Louis Sachar.

Lesson 1

✦ Before students have begun reading the book, have them complete "Judging a Book" (page 8).

✦ Read "About the Author" (page 7) to the students. Have a discussion with students about their expectations for the novel based on the book's cover and what they know about its author.

✦ Complete "'C' Where You Stand" (page 9).

✦ Introduce the concept of Interactive Novel Logs (see page 5). Prepare a blank notebook for each student or allow students to prepare their own.

Lesson 2

✦ Read Section I (Chapters 1–7) of the novel.

✦ See Section I "Teacher Instructions" (page 16). Have students add to their Interactive Novel Logs and complete the other Section I activities.

Lesson 3

✦ Read Section II (Chapters 8–19) of the novel.

✦ See Section II "Teacher Instructions" (page 22). Have students add to their Interactive Novel Logs and complete the other Section II activities.

Lesson 4

✦ Read Section III (Chapters 20–28) of the novel.

✦ See Section III "Teacher Instructions" (page 28). Have students add to their Interactive Novel Logs and complete the other Section III activities.

Lesson 5

✦ Read Section IV (Chapters 29–32) of the novel.

✦ See Section IV "Teacher Instructions" (page 35). Have students add to their Interactive Novel Logs and complete the other Section IV activities.

Lesson 6

✦ Read Section V (Chapters 33–42) of the novel.

✦ See Section V "Teacher Instructions" (page 41). Have students add to their Interactive Novel Logs and complete the other Section V activities.

Lesson 7

✦ Read Section VI (Chapters 43–50) of the novel.

✦ See Section VI "Teacher Instructions" (page 47). Have students add to their Interactive Novel Logs and complete the other Section VI activities.

Lesson 8

✦ Consult "Teacher Instructions" for the Post-Reading Activities (page 54). Synthesize understanding by completing the first two of these activities (pages 55–58).

✦ Allow students to reimagine and add to the text by completing "A New Point of View" (page 60), "Considering Genre" (page 61), and "Filling in the Holes" (pages 62–63).

✦ Complete larger-scale collaborative (pages 59, 64–69) and individual (70–71) projects.

✦ Have students share final thoughts and opinions on the novel by using the last two Post-Reading Activities (pages 72–73).

✦ Consider additional vocabulary-based activities (pages 74–75).

NOVEL INFORMATION

Book Summary

Stanley Yelnats IV has always had bad luck. So has his father before him and his father's father before him. It's all due to Stanley's no-good-dirty-rotten-pig-stealing-great-great-grandfather, or so the story goes. With equal parts humor and humanity, *Holes* tells the tale of cursed people and the cursed town where it all began and it all continues.

Stanley finds himself detained in the scorching hot and inappropriately named Camp Green Lake, punished for a crime he didn't commit. His sentence: he must dig an enormous hole each and every day for 18 months. While doing this, he must also navigate the politics, personalities, and perils of the other inmates, the counselors, the local wildlife, and a menacing figure known as the Warden. What is the Warden hoping to find in these holes? What secrets are buried in a place where rain hasn't fallen in over 100 years? What events brought down a thriving town, and what can possibly be done to reverse the curse? Louis Sachar reveals all of this and more in a novel about the causes of destiny and the effects that connect every character, every action, every time, and every place.

About the Author

Louis Sachar's interest in writing for children began in college. He earned credit helping out at Hillside Elementary in Northern California, and he became known to the kids there as "Louis the Yard Teacher." His experiences inspired him to write *Sideways Stories from Wayside School*. In all, Sachar has written five books about Wayside, an elementary school where supernatural occurrences are the norm.

Published in 1998, *Holes* is still Sachar's most decorated novel. It was awarded the 1998 U.S. National Book Award for Young People's Literature and the 1999 Newbery Award. Sachar has written two follow-ups to *Holes*: 2003's *Stanley Yelnats' Survival Guide to Camp Green Lake* and 2006's *Small Steps*, which checks in on such characters from *Holes* as Armpit and X-Ray.

Make It a Text Set!

The following novels can form ideal text sets with *Holes*. (**Note:** Vet books in advance to ensure they are appropriate for your students.)

Other Books by Louis Sachar	Books by Other Authors
Sideways Stories from Wayside School (1978)	*Hoot* by Carl Hiaasen
Stanley Yelnats' Survival Guide to Camp Green Lake (2003)	*Wonder* by R.J. Palacio
Small Steps (2006)	

NAME: _____

JUDGING A BOOK

You are about to read a novel named *Holes*. Before you even pick up the book and look at it, answer these questions.

1. Have you heard of this novel before? ☐ YES ☐ NO

   If **YES**, then explain what you have heard or already know about this novel.

   _____

   _____

2. Think about the title of the book. Based on the title *Holes*, what do you expect the tone of the novel to be? Place a checkmark next to any or all.

   ☐ adventurous   ☐ funny   ☐ heartwarming   ☐ sad

   ☐ scary   ☐ silly   ☐ heartbreaking   ☐ tense

   Explain your choice(s) here.

   _____

   _____

Now pick up the book. You have probably heard the saying, "Don't judge a book by its cover," but let's do it anyway.

3. Briefly describe the colors on the front of the book.

   _____

   _____

4. Briefly describe the images on the front of the book.

   _____

   _____

   _____

5. In a few sentences, describe the mood evoked by the color and images on the front of the book. In other words, based on these two elements, what impressions and feelings do you have about the book you are about to read?

   _____

   _____

   _____

   _____

NAME: _____

"C" WHERE YOU STAND

Each reader begins a book with his or her own ideas, opinions, and tidbits of knowledge. *Holes* is a book that explores many ideas and topics. Just a few are listed below. For each one, write a little about the ideas you are bringing with you as you begin the journey of reading this novel.

Camps

✦ If a place has the word "Camp" in its name, what kinds of things do you expect it to have? What things do you picture when you hear about a place with "Camp" in its name?

_____

_____

_____

Crime

✦ What kinds of punishment should minors (children) get for stealing and other crimes? Is it right or wrong to make them do hard labor (work) to pay off their debts to society? If so, why? If not, what would be a more fitting punishment? Explain.

_____

_____

_____

Class

✦ Do you believe that a person's wealth (or lack of it) affects how he or she is treated in the judicial (court) system? Explain.

_____

_____

_____

Curses

✦ Do you believe in curses? Do you believe that people can be destined to have bad luck based on things that happened in their past or in their family's past? Explain.

_____

_____

_____

NAME: _____

WHAT HAPPENED WHEN?

Holes tells multiple stories and spans many generations of characters. Most of these plot lines are either about Stanley's family or about the goings-on at Camp Green Lake.

After each section of *Holes*, think about each major event described. Was the event mostly about Camp Green Lake, or was it mostly about Stanley's family? When did the event take place? Use the chart below to **categorize** and **summarize** each major event.

✦ **categorize** = put into the correct category

✦ **summarize** = give a very brief description of what happened

+ +

Summary for Section #: _____   **Chapters in this section:** _____

Page numbers in this section: *from page* _____ *to page* _____

+ +

Camp Green Lake (Now)	Camp Green Lake (In the Past)
Stanley's Family (Recently)	**Stanley's Family (Long Ago)**

NAME: _____

A DYNAMIC PROTAGONIST

A character can be **static** or **dynamic**. A **static character** does not change. Static characters act and think the same throughout the novel. However, **dynamic characters** change in some way, maybe even more than one way. In many novels, the **protagonist**, or main character, is a dynamic character, and the way this character changes is connected to the theme of the novel.

As you read each section of *Holes*, examine the characterization of Stanley carefully. Consider his thoughts, beliefs, and actions. For each section, think about which **character traits** stand out. A character trait is a descriptive word that identifies a quality about the character, like *happy*, *selfish*, *rude*, or *thoughtful*. As you continue reading, look for ways Stanley changes.

+ +

Section #: _____   **Chapters in this section:** _____

Page numbers in this section: *from page* _____ *to page* _____

+ +

What two character traits stand out the most in this section? Fill out the chart below. Name the two traits. Then give an example from this section that shows each of the traits you identified.

	Trait #1	Trait #2
Stanley is . . .		
Example from this section		

What about Stanley changes during this section of the novel? Give two examples. They can be about Stanley's thoughts, feeling, actions, physical appearance, etc.

	Example #1	Example #2
Changes		
Why do you think he changes in this way?		

NAME: _____

MAJOR MINORS

Holes has one major character. His name is Stanley, and much of the novel's plot revolves around his experiences before and during his time at Camp Green Lake. However, the novel has many minor characters. These characters are important, too.

Fill out the chart below with information about each character. Only include information from the section you have just read. Does this section give you any ideas about why the author included this character in the book? How in this section does this character add to the themes of the novel or give us more insight into the character of Stanley?

✦ ✦

Section #: _____   **Chapters in this section:** _____

Page numbers in this section: *from page* _____ *to page* _____

✦ ✦

Character's Name	Information and Ideas
The Warden	
Mr. Sir	
Mr. Pendanski	
X-Ray	
Zero	
Kate Barlow	

Complete the same type of chart for any of Stanley's ancestors (father, great-great-grandfather, etc.) who appear in this section.

Name	Relation to Stanley	Information and Ideas

ALL TYPES OF TROUBLE

Over the course of *Holes*, Stanley Yelnats IV goes through a lot of difficulties. He is caught up in one conflict after another. A conflict is a struggle against something or someone.

There are many types of conflict that can occur in literature. Three main types are . . .

+ **Person vs. Person** — Another person or group causes trouble for a character.

+ **Person vs. Self** — A character's emotions, thoughts, or feelings cause him/her trouble.

+ **Person vs. Nature** — Something in nature causes trouble for a character.

In the section you have just read, find at least one example of each type of conflict that Stanley faces. Cite evidence from the story for each example you provide.

+ +

Section #: _____   **Chapters in this section:** _____

Page numbers in this section: *from page* _____ *to page* _____

+ +

Person vs. Person	Person vs. Self	Person vs. Nature
Example:	Example:	Example:
Quotation that shows this conflict:	Quotation that shows this conflict:	Quotation that shows this conflict:
Page number(s):	Page number(s):	Page number(s):

NAME: _____

CHOICE WORDS

+ +

Word from Novel: _____ **From Chapter #:** _____

+ +

1. Find one quotation in which this word appears in the novel. Write it in the box.

   [ ]

2. Reread the paragraph or section that contains the challenge word. Consider what is happening in the story and how the author uses the word. This information can help you figure out its meaning. Based on the words and ideas around the challenge word, what do you think is its meaning?

   _____

   _____

3. Explain why you think this is the meaning of the word, based on the context.

   _____

   _____

   _____

4. Now look up the word in the dictionary and write down the definition of this word that best fits the way it is used in the novel.

   _____

   _____

5. What is the part of speech of this word as it is used in the novel? _____

6. Next, look up the word in the thesaurus and write at least one synonym and one antonym of the word.

   Synonym(s): _____   Antonym(s): _____

   _____   _____

7. Write your own sentence that uses the vocabulary word.

   _____

   _____

CRYSTAL BALL

Now that you have read this section, where do you think the story will go next? Make two predictions based on what you have read so far. They can be about any of the following:

✦ **plot** — What will happen next in the story (either in the present time or the past)?

✦ **characterization** — What changes will Stanley or other characters undergo?

✦ **theme** — What big ideas about life, people, etc., will the author explore?

Use details from previous sections to explain why you are making each prediction.

+ +

Section #: _____   **Chapters in this section:** _____

Page numbers in this section: *from page* _____ *to page* _____

+ +

I predict this will happen:

Here is why I predict this:

_____

I predict this will happen:

Here is why I predict this:

TEACHER INSTRUCTIONS

This first section of *Holes* introduces us to a place with no hope, a character who has been wrongly punished, and a past where an honest mistake has led to a century of bad luck.

After your students have read Chapters 1–7, have them begin their analyses of this section of the novel by completing the following activities for their Interactive Novel Logs. Each of these activities is to be done individually.

+ **"What Happened When?" on page 10.** Instruct students that their summaries should be brief and include only the most important details.

+ **"A Dynamic Protagonist" on page 11.** Be sure the students understand the concept of *dynamic* vs. *static* before beginning this activity.

+ **"Major Minors" on page 12.** Read the directions to students before beginning.

+ **"All Types of Trouble" on page 13.** Before beginning, provide examples of each type of conflict.

+ **"Choice Words" on page 14.** Assign one or more words from "Novel Vocabulary" (page 75) or allow students to choose their own word(s).

+ +

Students will then further examine this section through the following worksheets:

Activity: "The Parts of *Holes*"   **Page #:** 17
Focus: Craft and Structure   **Learning Type:** Individual
Description: Look at beginnings, endings, and lengths to examine the way the author breaks the novel into chapters and what effect these elements have on the reader.

Activity: "Setting the Mood"   **Page #:** 18
Focus: Setting   **Learning Type:** Individual
Description: Consider how the author introduces the main setting of *Holes* and examine the roles it plays in setting up the tone of the novel.

Activity: "Tone vs. Mood"   **Page #:** 19
Focus: Craft and Structure   **Learning Type:** Collaborative
Description: With partners, analyze the similarities and differences between the tone and mood of the stories.

Activity: "Then and Now"   **Page #:** 20
Focus: Plot, Craft and Structure   **Learning Type:** Individual
Description: Compare and contrast the two storylines found in Chapter 7.

Activity: "Section I Log-In"   **Page #:** 21
Focus: Plot, etc.   **Learning Type:** Individual
Description: Complete "Crystal Ball" worksheets in order to predict future events in the novel. Then choose from several options to add to Interactive Novel Logs.

NAME: _____

THE PARTS OF *HOLES*

The novel *Holes* is divided into many chapters. Think about how and why the author broke up the story in this section of the novel in this way.

The Beginnings

Each chapter begins with a sentence that the author hopes will make the reader want to read further into the chapter. Choose a beginning of one of the chapters in this section (Chapters 1–7). Quote the sentence and then explain why it made you want to read more.

Quote: _____

Why It's Effective: _____

_____

The Endings

Each chapter ends with a sentence that the author hopes will make the reader want to flip to the next chapter and continue reading the novel. Choose an ending of one of the chapters in this section (Chapters 1–7). Quote the sentence and then explain why it was effective in making you want to immediately read the next chapter.

Quote: _____

Why It's Effective: _____

_____

The Lengths

The chapters in *Holes* are not all the same length. Some are very short, while others are fairly long. Choose one of each—a short chapter and a long one—and explain why each had to be the length it was.

Chapter # _____ is short. The reason for this is _____

_____

Chapter # _____ is long. The reason for this is _____

_____

What effect did reading chapters of different lengths have on you as the reader? How did it help/hurt your enjoyment of the novel?

_____

_____

NAME: _____

SETTING THE MOOD

In literature, the **setting** is *where* and/or *when* the story takes place. A novel's **mood** is the feelings and emotions it gives the reader. Answer the questions below to examine these key elements in *Holes*.

1. How does the novel begin? Who or what is first introduced?

_____

2. List some words and phrases the author uses in this introduction.

_____

_____

_____

3. Based on these words and phrases, what *mood* is given to the reader? Explain.

_____

_____

_____

4. Why do you think the novel begins by introducing a place instead of a person? As a reader, for what do you think this beginning might prepare you?

_____

_____

_____

_____

5. In your opinion, what are the three worst things about Camp Green Lake? Put them in order from bad to worst. Use examples from the novel to explain why each belongs on your list.

Bad: _____

Why? _____

Worse: _____

Why? _____

The Worst: _____

Why? _____

NAME(S): _____

TONE VS. MOOD

On the previous worksheet, you focused a bit on the mood of the first section of *Holes*. Tone is a bit different than **mood**.

✦ A novel's **tone** is the author's attitude toward the subject about which he or she is writing.

✦ A novel's **mood** is the feeling and emotions it gives to the reader.

+ +

Begin by checking all of the answers you feel correctly answer this question: *Based on Chapters 1–7, what is the <u>tone</u> of Louis Sachar's novel?*

❑ harsh   ❑ light   ❑ sly   ❑ passionate   ❑ ironic

❑ gentle   ❑ heavy   ❑ angry   ❑ relaxed   ❑ straightforward

Decide who will be Partner #1 and who will be Partner #2. Follow the instructions below to have a discussion about the tone and mood of the novel.

Partner #1's Name: _____   **Partner #2's Name:** _____

First	Take turns explaining your choices with your partner. Each partner should reveal two answers and use examples from Chapter 1–7 to explain those choices.
Next	Partner #1 should answer this question aloud: *How are the tone and mood of Chapters 1–7 similar?* Partner #2 should listen to Partner #1's answer and repeat it aloud to his or her partner.
Then	Partner #2 should answer this question aloud: *How are the tone and mood of Chapters 1–7 different?* Partner #1 should listen to Partner #2's answer and repeat it aloud to his or her partner.
Finally	Work together to answer this question: *Are the tone and the mood more similar or different?* In other words, does the author's feeling about the characters, events, and settings of the novel seem to be more similar to or different from the emotions you feel as you read the novel? Write your answers on the lines below.

_____

_____

_____

_____

THEN AND NOW

Chapter 7 is the longest chapter of this first part of the book. The action in this chapter follows two storylines, one that happens in the present and one that happens in the past. Give a brief summary of the actions described in this chapter.

	In the Present	In the Past
Characters Involved		
Actions that Occur		

1. Compare the two storylines.

	The Present	The Past
a. Which one had more action and events?	❑	❑
b. Which one gave the most background information?	❑	❑
c. Which one took place over a longer span of time?	❑	❑

2. Why do you think the author chose to make one of the storylines less eventful than the other? How do the two storylines complement (add to and enrich) each other?

_____

_____

_____

_____

3. Based on what you read in Chapter 7, does Elya Yelnats deserve to be referred to as a no-good-dirty-rotten-pig-stealing-great-great-grandfather? Give reasons from the text to support your answer.

_____

_____

_____

_____

NAME: _____

SECTION I LOG-IN

Now that you have finished the activities for this section of *Holes*, take some time to add to your Interactive Novel Log before you begin reading the next section.

✦ **First, make predictions about what will happen next in the novel.**
   Use your "Crystal Ball" worksheet (page 15) to do this.

✦ **Next, make a more personal connection to what you have read.**
   Choose one of the suggestions below and use it to fill a page in your Interactive Novel Log. Take this opportunity to connect with the novel in a way that appeals to you.

✦ ✦

Ideas for Your Interactive Novel Log

1
Why's It Named That?

The name of Camp Green Lake is ironic: there's no lake, nothing is green, and most people would think that something called "camp" should be fun. Have you ever come across a person, place, or thing that was ironically named—in other words, its name suggested it would be the opposite of what it really was? Devote a page in your Novel Log to this curiously named thing.

2
Place and Time

Stanley didn't really steal anything; he was just in the wrong place at the wrong time. This happens to him a lot. Has this ever happened to you? Or, has the opposite happened? Have you ever just happened to be in the right place at the right time? Use your page to describe this event and the results that came from it.

3
Truly Great Great-Grandparent

Stanley's family has had their share of bad luck, all of which they blame on Stanley's great-great-grandfather. Many people, however, have their ancestors (grandparents, great-grandparents, etc.) to thank for the life they have. Devote a page to one or more of your ancestors. Give details about what they did (hard work, immigrating to this country, moving to this city, etc.) that made life better for your family.

4
Not What It Seemed

Stanley's great-great-grandfather wanted nothing more than to marry Myra. However, once he was close to accomplishing his goal, he saw that marrying Myra would not be such a great thing after all. Write about something that you wanted really badly but that didn't turn out to be worth the trouble. If that has never happened to you, then write about why you really want something and why it will be worth the trouble once you get it.

TEACHER INSTRUCTIONS

In this section, Stanley learns more about the dynamics of his group at Camp Green Lake, and he discovers a mysterious object that gets the attention of the Warden.

After your students have read Chapters 8–19, have them begin their analyses of this section of the novel by completing the following activities for their Interactive Novel Logs. Each of these activities is to be done individually.

✦ **"What Happened When?"** (page 10)

✦ **"A Dynamic Protagonist"** (page 11)

✦ **"Major Minors"** (page 12)

✦ **"All Types of Trouble"** (page 13)

✦ **"Choice Words"** (page 14)

> For this section, distribute new copies of the Interactive Novel Log worksheets on pages 10–14.

+ +

Students will then further examine this section through the following worksheets:

Activity: "A Long Look at Lizards" **Page #:** 23
Focus: Plot, Craft **Learning Type:** Collaborative
Description: With partners, create a labeled drawing of a yellow-spotted lizard. Describe these creatures in detail and determine how their introduction might foreshadow future events in the novel.

Activity: "The Boys of Group D" **Page #:** 24–25
Focus: Plot **Learning Type:** Individual
Description: Consider the dynamics of Stanley's digging group and how those dynamics change due to the events in this section.

Activity: "Zero In" **Page #:** 26
Focus: Character, Craft **Learning Type:** Individual
Description: Rewrite a crucial scene from the point of view of another character. Explain how the character's voice is hinted at through details in the novel.

Activity: "Section II Log-In" **Page #:** 27
Focus: Plot, etc. **Learning Type:** Individual
Description: Complete "Crystal Ball" worksheets in order to predict future events in the novel. Then choose from several options to add to Interactive Novel Logs.

A LONG LOOK AT LIZARDS

This section of the novel begins with a chapter about Camp Green Lake's most dangerous inhabitant: the yellow-spotted lizard. Work with partners to create an encyclopedia entry on these creatures.

The Yellow-Spotted Lizard

Draw a picture of the creature here. Use arrows to label your picture and describe some of its most unusual physical features.

Write about the lizard here. Give details about its size, its diet, how it moves, where it lives, and what dangers it poses to humans.

_____

_____

_____

_____

_____

_____

_____

One literary device an author may use is **foreshadowing**. This is done when an author introduces something that will factor into the novel later in the plot.

1. Do you and your partner think Chapter 8 foreshadows events that will happen later in *Holes*? Give reasons for your answer.

   _____

   _____

   _____

2. In Chapter 8, the author gives us many details about these lizards. Which of these details most makes you think that we will read more about yellow-spotted lizards later in the novel? Why?

   _____

   _____

   _____

THE BOYS OF GROUP D

In this section of the novel, we learn a lot about the members of Stanley's group. Complete the worksheet below and on page 25 to look at each member and how they get along.

1. Fill in the chart to name each member of Stanley's digging group. Put them in order of how they stand in the drinking line in Chapter 10. Also give a brief description of each group member. (**Note:** Some of the characters' real names were given in earlier chapters. Some have not been given yet.)

Order	Nickname	Real Name	Brief Description
1			
2			
3			
4			
5			
6			
7			

2. Who appears to be the leader of the group? _____

   Give two reasons why Stanley thinks this person must be the leader.

   _____

   _____

   _____

3. What happens in the Wreck Room that makes Stanley first feel as though he has been accepted by the group?

   _____

   _____

   _____

THE BOYS OF GROUP D (CONT.)

4. In your opinion, how does Mr. Pendanski treat the group? Does he treat everyone in the group the same? Give specific examples to support your ideas.

_____

_____

_____

_____

5. Why does Stanley give the tube to X-Ray instead of showing it to Mr. Pendanski? Use a quotation from the novel to support your answer.

_____

_____

_____

Quotation: _____

_____ Page number: _____

6. Name two things that happen as a result of Stanley giving the tube to X-Ray.

_____

_____

_____

7. Why do you think Zigzag hits Stanley with the shovel? Give reasons from the novel to support your answer.

_____

_____

_____

8. Why do you think Stanley takes the blame for the sunflower seeds in Chapter 19? Do you think his experiences *before* Camp Green Lake are part of his decision to do this? Explain.

_____

_____

_____

_____

ZERO IN

Zero is a mysterious character. At this point, we have only been given a few hints about who he is and the troubles he has faced in his life.

Imagine you are Zero. What must he have felt and thought during the scene with the stolen sunflower seeds? What are his thoughts about Stanley taking the blame and being driven away by Mr. Sir? What are his feelings toward the rest of the group?

1. Rewrite this scene from Zero's perspective.

   ✦ Use the first-person point of view in your writing. (In other words, use the pronouns "I" and "me.")

   ✦ Write in Zero's "voice." What would it sound like if we could hear his thoughts?

_____

_____

_____

_____

_____

_____

_____

_____

_____

_____

_____

_____

_____

_____

2. Why did you write Zero's voice in this way? What details from *Holes* gave you a clear idea of how Zero might think?

_____

_____

_____

NAME: _____

SECTION II LOG-IN

Now that you have finished the activities for this section of *Holes*, take some time to add to your Interactive Novel Log before you begin reading the next section.

✦ **First, make predictions about what will happen next in the novel.**
Use your "Crystal Ball" worksheet (page 15) to do this.

✦ **Next, make a more personal connection to what you have read.**
Choose one of the suggestions below and use it to fill a page in your Interactive Novel Log. Take this opportunity to connect with the novel in a way that appeals to you.

+ +

Ideas for Your Interactive Novel Log

1
What's In a Name?

Nicknames are a part of life in Camp Green Lake. Divide your page in half. On one side, write about the nickname that is the best in your opinion. On the other side, write about the one that is the worst. You can choose from the nicknames of any of the campers or counselors. It is up to you to decide what makes a nickname good or bad. Explain why you feel this way.

2
The Hardest Hole

Throughout this section of the novel, there is a running joke about which hole is the hardest to dig. Is it the first hole? The second? Create a page that seriously (or jokingly) examines this question. Your page could be in the form of a science blog that determines once and for all which hole is the hardest. Or your page could be in the form of a cartoon or graph. There are many possibilities.

3
Pig Latin

In Chapter 11, X-Ray says that his nickname is the Pig Latin version of his real name. If you are unfamiliar with Pig Latin, do Internet research to find out how this made-up language works. Then create a 10-question quiz by writing the Pig Latin versions of the names of famous athletes, entertainers, etc. Create an answer key at the bottom of your page.

4
Could Be K.B.?

The tube that Stanley finds is engraved with the initials "K.B." Stanley thinks the tube might be a fancy pen, and the initials might belong to a famous author. But he doesn't know any authors with those initials. Write a list of all the people you know or have heard of who have the initials "K.B."

TEACHER INSTRUCTIONS

In this section, Stanley's actions lead to unintended consequences, and we learn the details of Green Lake's past.

After your students have read Chapters 20–28, have them begin their analyses of this section of the novel by completing the following activities for their Interactive Novel Logs. Each of these activities is to be done individually. Distribute new copies of each.

+ **"What Happened When?"** on page 10.
+ **"A Dynamic Protagonist"** on page 11.
+ **"Major Minors"** on page 12.
+ **"All Types of Trouble"** on page 13.
+ **"Choice Words"** on page 14.

+ +

Students will then further examine this section through the following worksheets:

Activity: "Chain of Events" **Page #:** 29
Focus: Plot **Learning Type:** Individual
Description: Examine cause and effect by looking at the event that ends Chapter 19 and the two sets of consequences that occur as a result.

Activity: "Speaking of the Warden" **Page #:** 30
Focus: Plot, Character **Learning Type:** Collaborative
Description: Practice speaking and listening skills by discussing the motives and actions of the Warden and determining how information about Green Lake's past might offer insight into her character.

Activity: "What It Really Means" **Page #:** 31
Focus: Craft, Inference **Learning Type:** Individual
Description: Examine how several chapters end with lines that hint at additional information. Locate an example in which the author ends a chapter by giving information more explicitly. Determine the reasoning for each choice.

Activity: "The Onion Man" **Page #:** 32
Focus: Plot, Character **Learning Type:** Individual
Description: Look closely at a minor character and determine his significance to the novel as a whole.

Activity: "The Antagonists" **Page #:** 33
Focus: Plot, Character, Craft **Learning Type:** Individual
Description: Consider the unsavory characters in the story of Green Lake's past. Determine the author's tone.

Activity: "Section III Log-In" **Page #:** 34
Focus: Plot, etc. **Learning Type:** Individual
Description: Complete "Crystal Ball" worksheets in order to predict future events in the novel. Then choose from several options to add to Interactive Novel Logs.

CHAINS OF EVENTS

Chapter 19 ends with the sunflower-seed incident. From that one event, two main sets of consequences are put into action. One involves Mr. Sir, while the other involves Zero.

Use the events from Chapters 20–28 to complete each chain below. In the first blank box in each chain, write what happens as an immediate result of what Stanley does at the end of Chapter 19. Then show how each result leads to another result, which leads to another. Continue in this way until you have completed each chain.

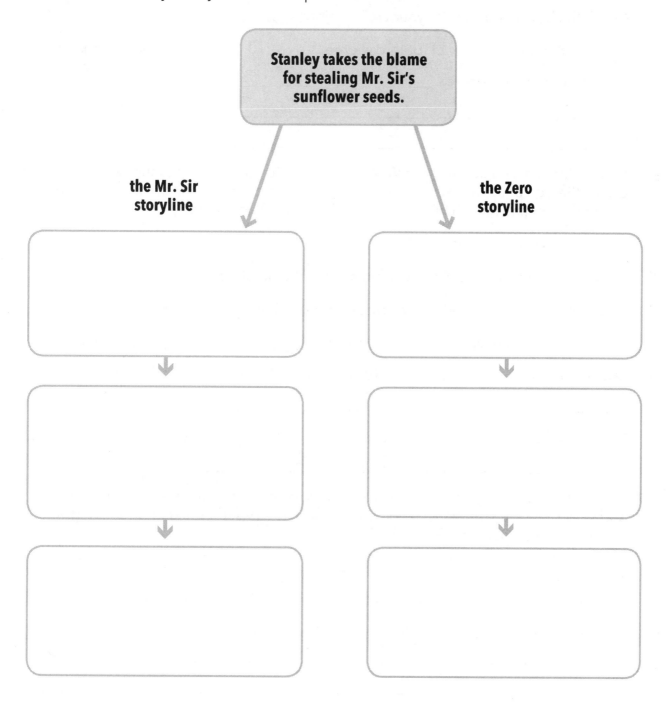

SPEAKING OF THE WARDEN

Discuss the following questions aloud with your partner. Be prepared to defend your answers in front of the class.

1. Do you and your partner agree or disagree with this statement?

> *The Warden does not punish Stanley for stealing (or lying about stealing)*
> *Mr. Sir's sunflower seeds.*

Check the box that describes your two opinions.

❑ both agree   ❑ both disagree   ❑ one agrees, one disagrees

Explain your opinions here: _____

_____

_____

2. What is the main reason why the Warden chooses to handle the situation in this way? Check the box of the answer that, in your opinion, is the best. (If you and your partner have different answers, then each one of you should check a box.)

❑ She is annoyed with Mr. Sir. for wasting her time.

❑ She wants to show Stanley what she is capable of doing.

❑ She wants to give Mr. Sir a reason to make Stanley's life miserable.

❑ She is still angry about the campers not digging up anything else like the tube.

Did you and your partner agree on the same answer to the above question? Explain.

_____

_____

_____

3. Do you think the story about Green Lake's past gives us any clues about the Warden and who she is? If so, what can you guess about her based on the information given in Chapters 23, 25, 26, and/or 28?

_____

_____

_____

_____

_____

NAME: _____

WHAT IT REALLY MEANS

Several of the chapters in this section of the novel end with lines that the reader must interpret. In each of these cases, not all of the information is given. The reader must use what he or she knows about the characters or plot of the novel to fill in the gaps and understand what is really being said.

Write down the last lines of the following chapters. For each, explain what has just happened leading up to that line. Lastly, write the implication of that line. In other words, what information can we infer or assume from this one line?

Chapter: ___20___ **Last Line:** _____

What has just happened? _____

_____

What is the implication? _____

_____

Chapter: ___21___ **Last Line:** _____

What has just happened? _____

_____

What is the implication? _____

_____

Find in this section of the novel another chapter that ends in a similar way. Explain why you feel the author made this choice and what effect it has on the reader at this point.

Chapter: _____ **Last Line:** _____

What has just happened? _____

What is the implication? _____

Then, find in this section a chapter that ends with explicit information—in other words, the author tells you exactly what is happening.

Chapter: _____ **Last Line:** _____

Why do you think the author gives this information in this way? _____

_____

NAME: _____

THE ONION MAN

Answer these questions to examine the character of Sam and his role in the plot of *Holes*.

1. In which chapter is Sam introduced? _____

2. What is the first thing we learn about Sam? _____

_____

3. Based on what you learn about Sam in Chapters 25 and 26, write three words that describe who he is as a person. (<u>Do not</u> choose words that describe his physical appearance.) For each word, give details from the novel to support your choice.

Word	Details

4. Why do you think Miss Katherine fell in love with Sam? What might her feelings toward Sam say about her as a person/character?

_____

_____

_____

_____

5. Sam is only alive for two chapters in *Holes*. Make the case why he is an important character in the novel.

_____

_____

_____

_____

_____

THE ANTAGONISTS

In literature, an **antagonist** is a person or force who opposes or threatens the **protagonist** (the main character). Answer these questions about Green Lake's past.

1. In this storyline of the events that took place over 100 years ago, who is the main protagonist?

   _____

2. Choose three characters who function as antagonists in this storyline. For each, describe the role he or she had in the awful facts described at the end Chapter 26.

Name of Antagonist	What He or She Did

3. Why do you think Miss Katherine specifically sought out the sheriff for revenge?

   _____

   _____

   _____

4. Why does Kissin' Kate Barlow die laughing? Use evidence to support your answer.

   _____

   _____

   _____

5. What is the author's tone when Trout Walker is being described? In other words, what are the author's feelings about this character? Use evidence from the novel to support your answer.

   _____

   _____

   _____

   _____

NAME: _____

SECTION III LOG-IN

Now that you have finished the activities for this section of *Holes*, take some time to add to your Interactive Novel Log before you begin reading the next section.

✦ **First, make a prediction about what will happen next in the novel.**

Use your "Crystal Ball" worksheet (page 15) to do this.

✦ **Next, make a more personal connection to what you have read.**

Choose one of the suggestions below and use it to fill a page in your Interactive Novel Log. Take this opportunity to connect with the novel in a way that appeals to you.

+ +

Ideas for Your Interactive Novel Log

1
A Sensitive Subject

Imagine that you are Mr. Pendanski. Carefully craft a letter or e-mail to Mr. Sir. Explain to him why you think he should stop depriving Stanley of water. Be careful, though! You know that Mr. Sir is angry about this issue. You must word your letter in a way that does not upset him and convinces him to change his actions.

2
Teaching Reading

Zero asks Stanley to teach him how to read. What if you were asked to do this for someone? How would you go about it? Give a plan with at least five steps. Show how you would teach someone to read. What tools would you use? How long do you think it would take?

3
An Onion a Day

Sam believes that onions are a miracle food that prolongs life and health. What if this were absolutely true? How would you and your family get more onions in your diet? Write a few recipes that include onions. Or, use your page to explain why you would not eat onions no matter how much health they could bring you.

4
Better Than Spiced Peaches

All of Green Lake seems to agree that Miss Katherine's spiced peaches are the town's greatest food. What is the greatest food in your town or city? Who makes it, and why is it so good? Write a food review devoted to this local treat. If possible, include photos of the place where this food is made and of the food itself.

34

TEACHER INSTRUCTIONS

In this section, Zero and Stanley each make dramatic choices that will put them in harm's way, and Stanley's family's past offers him a glimmer of hope in a desert of regret.

After your students have read Chapters 29–32, have them begin their analyses of this section of the novel by completing the following activities for their Interactive Novel Logs. Each of these activities is to be done individually.

✦ **"What Happened When?"** on page 10.

✦ **"A Dynamic Protagonist"** on page 11.

✦ **"Major Minors"** on page 12.

✦ **"All Types of Trouble"** on page 13.

✦ **"Choice Words"** on page 14.

For this section, distribute new copies of the Interactive Novel Log worksheets on pages 10–14.

✦ ✦

Students will then further examine this section through the following worksheets:

Activity: "All Kinds of Unkind"   **Page #:** 36–37
Focus: Plot, Character   **Learning Type:** Individual
Description: Examine how certain characters treat other characters and determine their motivations for doing so.
(Extra Idea: After students have completed their worksheets, take a class poll to reveal their answers to question #9. Have students use this data to create bar graphs. If necessary, show students examples of bar graphs to ensure they understand how to create one.)

Activity: "The New Kid"   **Page #:** 38
Focus: Plot, Character   **Learning Type:** Individual
Description: Consider the camp's newest member and how he becomes an unlikely influence on the events of Chapter 32. Craft tweets about the day from this camper's perspective.

Activity: "Left in Suspense"   **Page #:** 39
Focus: Plot, Craft   **Learning Type:** Individual
Description: Look closely at how this section of the novel ends and how the author employs a cliffhanger to keep readers in suspense.

Activity: "Section IV Log-In"   **Page #:** 40
Focus: Plot, etc.   **Learning Type:** Individual
Description: Complete "Crystal Ball" worksheets in order to predict future events in the novel. Then choose from several options to add to Interactive Novel Logs.

NAME: _____

ALL KINDS OF UNKIND

One theme of this section of the novel seems to be of certain characters treating other characters unkindly. Take a closer look at these characters and try to determine why they treat others so meanly.

1. By what name do all of the campers call Hector Zeroni? _____

2. By what name does Mr. Pendanski call Hector Zeroni? _____

3. Look at your answer to #2. Why is this information unusual or noteworthy?

   _____

   _____

4. What do you think this says about Mr. Pendanski's view of Hector?

   _____

   _____

   As evidence to support your answer, provide two quotations from the novel.

   Quotation: _____

   _____ Page #: _____

   Quotation: _____

   _____ Page #: _____

5. In Chapter 30, Zigzag starts pushing Stanley. This is not the first time he has been aggressive toward Stanley. What does he do to Stanley earlier in the novel?

   _____

   _____

6. Why do you think he is so confrontational toward Stanley? Try to provide evidence from the novel to support your reason.

   _____

   _____

   _____

7. Now think back to earlier in the novel. What is the main reason why the townspeople of Green Lake are upset when Miss Katherine and Sam kiss?

   _____

   _____

ALL KINDS OF UNKIND (CONT.)

8. What might have been another reason why Trout Walker was upset about that kiss? Provide a quotation from the novel to support your answer.

_____

Quotation: _____

_____ Page #: _____

9. Of the three characters discussed on this worksheet, which one's motivation do you understand the least? In other words, which one seems to treat another character badly for very little reason? Check one of the answers listed. On the lines below, explain your answer and try to offer an explanation for the character's actions.

   ❑ Mr. Pendanski   ❑ Zigzag   ❑ Trout Walker

_____

_____

_____

_____

10. Why do you think the author chose to not give more explanation for this character's behavior?

_____

_____

+ +

Class Results

After you have completed your worksheet, your teacher will take a poll of the class to determine everyone's answer to #9. Use this data to create a bar graph.

# of Students	2	4	6	8	10	12	14	16	18	20	22	24
Mr. Pendanski												
Zigzag												
Trout Walker												

Did you find anything about the results of the class poll to be surprising? Explain.

_____

_____

NAME: _____

THE NEW KID

Chapter 32 introduces us to a new character. He may be a very minor character, but he does play a part in the events of this important chapter.

The New Member of Group D

Real Name: _____

Nickname: _____

Crime(s): _____

What part does this character play in Stanley's actions at the end of Chapter 32?

1. In what way does he plant the seed *before* Stanley's actions?

_____

_____

2. In what way does he help Stanley *during* these actions?

_____

_____

+ +

Imagine that this new member of Group D has access to a computer, and he likes to tweet about his daily adventures. Write three tweets (no more than 140 characters each) from throughout his first full day at Camp Green Lake. How would this character describe the events of that day from his perspective?

1.

2.

3.

NAME: _____

LEFT IN SUSPENSE

In literature, a cliffhanger is an ending—usually to a chapter—that leaves many questions unanswered and puts the readers in a state of suspense. What will happen next? There's only one thing to do: keep reading to find out. However, before you do that, let's take a look at how this cliffhanger works and why it is such an effective device for an author to use.

1. As Stanley heads out into the desert in search of Zero, what things give him hope that the situation will turn out okay? What things make the situation seem hopeless? After you complete your list, circle the column in which you wrote more things.

Give Him Hope	Make Him Feel Hopeless

2. Look at the last sentence of Chapter 32. What does the pronoun "it" stand for?

_____

3. What are the last three words of this sentence? _____

4. Why do you think the author repeats the final word of the chapter? How does this choice make you, the reader, feel when you read it?

_____
_____
_____

5. Stanley thinks this is the "stupidest thing" he has ever done. Without knowing what will happen next, do you think this is true? Pick a side, and write a paragraph to Stanley. Either agree or disagree with what he says. Give reasons for your opinion.

_____
_____
_____
_____
_____

NAME: _____

SECTION IV LOG-IN

Now that you have finished the activities for this section of *Holes*, take some time to add to your Interactive Novel Log before you begin reading the next section.

✦ **First, make a prediction about what will happen next in the novel.**

Use your "Crystal Ball" worksheet (page 15) to do this.

✦ **Next, make a more personal connection to what you have read.**

Choose one of the suggestions below and use it to fill a page in your Interactive Novel Log. Take this opportunity to connect with the novel in a way that appeals to you.

+ +

Ideas for Your Interactive Novel Log

1
God's Thumb

As a storm brews in the distance in Chapter 29, Stanley thinks he sees an unusual rock formation at the peak of a mountain. This reminds him of something his great-grandfather once said. Draw a picture of what Stanley sees. Use the imagery the author provides to lend details to your drawing.

2
Calendar Page

Create a calendar page for Stanley's stay at Camp Green Lake. Use the dates provided in Chapter 30 to show the three months that Stanley has been there. Write Xs or in some way keep track of the holes Stanley has dug. Is Zero's math accurate? If you can figure out on which days certain events occurred during Stanley's stay, then write those on your calendar, as well.

3
Unpleasant Conversation

Chapter 31 ends with Stanley overhearing a conversation that he knows is bad for Zero. In our lives, we sometimes overhear conversations of people speaking badly about other people or planning to do bad things. What is the best way to handle this situation? Write about an experience you've had or create a realistic experience that is similar to Stanley's. What did or would you do or say? Did you or would you confront those who are speaking?

4
The Most You've Ever Done

As Chapter 32 ends, Stanley believes he has just done something that is dumber than anything he's ever done before. Use your page to write about or draw pictures of the stupidest (or smartest, bravest, kindest, meanest, most unbelievable, etc.) thing you've ever done.

TEACHER INSTRUCTIONS

In this section, Stanley treks across the desert, finds Zero, and the two make their way up to God's Thumb.

After your students have read Chapters 33–42, have them begin their analyses of this section of the novel by completing the following activities for their Interactive Novel Logs. Each of these activities is to be done individually.

✦ **"What Happened When?"** on page 10.

✦ **"A Dynamic Protagonist"** on page 11.

✦ **"Major Minors"** on page 12.

✦ **"All Types of Trouble"** on page 13.

✦ **"Choice Words"** on page 14.

> For this section, distribute new copies of the Interactive Novel Log worksheets on pages 10-14.

Students will then further examine this section through the following worksheets:

Activity: "Desert Decisions"
Focus: Plot, Character, Setting
Page #: 42
Learning Type: Individual
Description: Analyze the decisions Stanley must make as he walks across the desert, first by himself and then with Zero.

Activity: "Scavenger Hunt"
Focus: Plot
Page #: 43
Learning Type: Collaborative
Description: With partners, locate things and ideas that were mentioned earlier in the novel and then show up during Stanley and Zero's trek through the desert. Discuss the importance of these things to the novel as a whole.

Activity: "A Tale of Two"
Focus: Character, Craft
Page #: 44
Learning Type: Individual
Description: Examine the two characters who are the sole focus of this section of the novel. Determine why the author chose to include only one brief scene involving other characters.

Activity: "A Change in Stanley"
Focus: Plot, Character
Page #: 45
Learning Type: Individual
Description: Closely read the final portion of Chapter 42. Use textual evidence to determine the reasons for Stanley's new mood and the pros and cons of the plan he is about to put in place.

Activity: "Section V Log-In"
Focus: Plot, etc.
Page #: 46
Learning Type: Individual
Description: Complete "Crystal Ball" worksheets in order to predict future events in the novel. Then choose from several options to add to Interactive Novel Logs.

NAME: _____

DESERT DECISIONS

As Stanley walks away from the camp, he sees what appears to be an unending stretch of desert before him. He knows that his immediate future will be filled with tough decisions.

1. What does Stanley realize about how far he can walk into the desert? Explain his thought process.

_____

_____

_____

2. As Stanley walks, what does he notice about this stretch of desert? How is it different from the landscape around Camp Green Lake?

_____

_____

_____

3. Once he finds Zero, the two of them must decide what to do next. What are Stanley's reasons for feeling that he and Zero must go back to Camp Green Lake?

_____

_____

4. What are Zero's reasons for being so certain that he will not go back to the camp?

_____

_____

5. Why do you think Stanley ultimately decides to move forward instead of turning back toward the camp?

_____

_____

_____

6. As this section ends, what decision does Stanley make? Why do you think he makes this decision at this time?

_____

_____

_____

NAME(S): _____

SCAVENGER HUNT

Now that you have finished this section of *Holes*, take some time to add to your Interactive Novel Logs.

In this section of the novel, we read about many objects and other things that remind us of storylines from earlier in the novel. Meet with your partner and discuss Stanley and Zero's journey across the desert and up the mountain. Together, find at least five things or ideas that we have read about in the earlier parts of the book.

Thing or Idea	Where We First Read About It

+ +

Practice Speaking and Listening!

Now that you have completed the chart together, discuss the following questions. Begin by deciding who will be Speaker 1 and who will be Speaker 2.

Speaker 1: _____
(name)

Speaker 2: _____
(name)

Answer this question aloud and support your opinion with reasons:

The most useful thing Zero came across in the desert was _____. This is because _____.

Listen to Speaker 1's answer and either agree or disagree with it. Give reasons for your opinion.

then

Answer this question aloud and support your opinion with reasons:

The most useful thing Stanley came across in the desert was _____. This is because _____.

Listen to Speaker 2's answer and either agree or disagree with it. Give reasons for your opinion.

NAME: _____

A TALE OF TWO

During this section, the focus of the novel narrows down to mostly two characters. Think about those two characters who are fighting for survival in harsh conditions.

1. Think about the lives these two characters have led up until this point.

	Stanley	Zero
What in this character's life has prepared him for this journey?		
Provide a quotation to support your reason.		
Page number		

2. These two characters must rely on each other to survive. Give at least two ways that each character helps the other to survive.

Stanley helps Zero	Zero helps Stanley

3. At this point in the novel, which of the two characters do you think is better equipped for making this journey? _____

Do you think you would have given the same answer after reading only the first few chapters of the novel? Explain and give an example from the novel.

_____
_____
_____

4. The chapters in this section focus almost entirely on these two characters. There is only one scene that does not feature these two. What happens in this scene?

_____
_____

Why do you think the author included this scene? _____

_____

A CHANGE IN STANLEY

As Chapter 42 ends, Stanley experiences feelings he hasn't had in a long time. A change comes over him. Reread the final part of the chapter (beginning with "Two nights later . . .") and answer the questions below.

1. What are Stanley's feelings at the end of Chapter 42? Describe his mood.

_____

_____

Provide a quotation to support your answer. _____

_____ Page #: _____

2. What are Stanley's thoughts about his change in mood? Why does he think he might be experiencing these feelings?

_____

_____

Provide a quotation to support your answer. _____

_____ Page #: _____

3. What are your thoughts about Stanley's change in mood? Why do you think he is experiencing these feelings at this point in the novel?

_____

_____

4. What is Stanley's plan as the chapter ends?

_____

_____

_____

5. What about his plan seems to excite him? What about his plan seems to trouble him?

Exciting	Troubling

NAME: _____

SECTION V LOG-IN

Now that you have finished the activities for this section of *Holes*, take some time to add to your Interactive Novel Log before you begin reading the next section.

✦ **First, make a prediction about what will happen next in the novel.**

Use your "Crystal Ball" worksheet (page 15) to do this.

✦ **Next, make a more personal connection to what you have read.**

Choose one of the suggestions below and use it to fill a page in your Interactive Novel Log. Take this opportunity to connect with the novel in a way that appeals to you.

+ +

Ideas for Your Interactive Novel Log

1
Knowing You're Halfway

As Stanley walks through the desert, he realizes that he can't walk for as long as his strength allows. Instead, he can only walk *halfway* as long as that. After all, he will need enough strength to walk back. Put yourself in Stanley's shoes. How do you think you would know that you've walked about halfway as far as you can? What clues would tell you that it's time to turn around? What would be your plan if you were in Stanley's position?

2
Indelible Image

An indelible image is a picture that sticks with you, one that you'll remember for quite a while. This section of *Holes* contains many descriptions of nature and of the harsh landscape of the desert and mountains. Which image or images from Stanley and Zero's journey stick with you the most? Draw one or more. Explain why this image is so indelible for you.

3
Stanley's Song

Stanley's family has a song that has been in their family for generations. Write the lyrics to this song somewhere on your page. Then analyze the lyrics. Decide what they mean and why this particular song might appeal to the Yelnats family.

4
That's Incredible!

When Stanley retraces his path down the mountain, he is shocked by how far he was able to carry Zero. The feat seems incredible to him. Have you ever done anything that you found amazing or unbelievable? Or, have you seen someone else do something that seemed impossible? Use the format of a newspaper article or online blog to write about this event.

TEACHER INSTRUCTIONS

In this section, the novel concludes with a complete reversal of Stanley's fortune as he and Zero recover the treasure, triumph over the Warden, and leave Camp Green Lake once and for all.

After your students have read Chapters 43–50, have them begin their analyses of this section of the novel by completing the following activities for their Interactive Novel Logs. Each of these activities is to be done individually. Distribute new copies of each.

✦ **"What Happened When?"** on page 10.

✦ **"A Dynamic Protagonist"** on page 11.

✦ **"Major Minors"** on page 12.

✦ **"All Types of Trouble"** on page 13.

✦ **"Choice Words"** on page 14.

✦ ✦

Students will then further examine this section through the following worksheets:

Activity: "The Return to Camp"   **Page #:** 48
Focus: Plot, Character, Craft   **Learning Type:** Individual
Description: Examine the changes in Stanley and Zero as they journey back to Camp Green Lake. Consider the author's inclusion of a sketch to illustrate their route.

Activity: "While They Were Gone"   **Page #:** 49
Focus: Plot, Cause and Effect   **Learning Type:** Individual
Description: Use clues from the novel to puzzle out the various events that took place while Stanley and Zero were away from Camp Green Lake. Determine the effects that resulted from this combination of events.

Activity: "Layer by Layer"   **Page #:** 50
Focus: Craft, Symbolism, Character   **Learning Type:** Collaborative
Description: Look closely at how onions function both literally–by explaining mysterious occurrences in the plot–and figuratively–as symbols.

Activity: "The Final Chapter"   **Page #:** 51
Focus: Plot, Craft   **Learning Type:** Individual
Description: Examine the ending of the novel. Explain the author's choices and offer opinions about those choices.

Activity: "Same Old Song?"   **Page #:** 52
Focus: Craft, Character   **Learning Type:** Individual
Description: Compare and contrast the lyrics to the songs sung by the Yelnats and Zeroni families.

Activity: "Section VI Log-In"   **Page #:** 53
Focus: Plot, etc.   **Learning Type:** Individual
Description: Complete "Crystal Ball" worksheets in order to predict future events in the novel. Then choose from several options to add to Interactive Novel Logs.

NAME: _____

THE RETURN TO CAMP

Chapter 43 describes Stanley and Zero's journey from God's Thumb back to camp.

1. Why are they returning to camp? What are they hoping to find/get there?

_____

_____

2. How would you describe how Stanley and Zero get along with each other during their journey back to camp? Cite evidence from the novel to support your answer. Give at least two examples.

_____

_____

_____

_____

3. Along the way, the two get a little lost. Zero draws a diagram to help Stanley understand that they are going the wrong way. In the space below, redraw Zero's diagram. Label each object and arrow.

4. This is the second time a drawing was included in the book. When was the first?

_____

Why do you think the author included these drawings in the novel?

_____

_____

5. What is the first clue that they are nearing the camp? What is the second clue?

_____

NAME: _____

WHILE THEY WERE GONE

Use the clues provided in the novel to piece together the events that transpired during Stanley and Zero's time near God's Thumb.

What happened . . .

to the members of Group D?	
to the theft case against Stanley?	
to Hector Zeroni's files?	
to Stanley's family?	

What does this combination of events add up to for Stanley and Zero? Explain what happens as a result of all these events.

_____

_____

_____

_____

_____

_____

NAME(S): _____

LAYER BY LAYER

In literature, a symbol is an object that represents something else. In this final section of *Holes*, one food source appears over and over again: the onion. Work with a partner to peel back the layers of this food source and see what it means to the novel as a whole.

Begin by deciding who will be Partner #1 and who will be Partner #2.

Partner #1's Name: _____   **Partner #2's Name:** _____

| **First** | Partner #1 asks this question: *How do onions save Stanley and Zero's lives while they are up in the hills near God's Thumb?* Partner #2 answers the question aloud. |

| **Next** | Partner #2 asks this question: *How do onions save their lives later in the story when they are in a hole near camp?* Partner #1 answers the question aloud. |

| **Then** | Partner #1 asks this question: *What story does the author insert at the beginning of Chapter 49?* Partner #2 answers the question aloud by giving details about the story. |

| **Finally** | Partner #2 asks this question: *What is the purpose of including this story at this point in the novel?* Partner #1 answers the question aloud by naming the important piece of information this story gives to the reader. |

+ +

Putting It All Together!

Answer the following questions together as a team.

1. Which character in the novel is most associated with onions? _____

2. How do onions and this character represent (stand for) similar ideas in the novel? What do they have in common?

   _____

   _____

3. How might onions symbolize the novel as a whole? (Hint: Think about what onions look like on the inside.)

   _____

   _____

   _____

   _____

NAME: _____

THE FINAL CHAPTER

In Chapter 50, the author chooses to give us information about some of the characters and places involved in the novel while not giving us information about others.

1. What happened to Camp Green Lake? _____

_____

_____

2. Why is this ironic or humorous? _____

_____

_____

3. What items were in the suitcase? _____

_____

_____

4. What does the author suggest was the real cause of the turnaround in fortune for Stanley, Zero, and their families?

_____

_____

_____

5. Explain the last page of the novel (beginning with the words, "A woman sitting in the chair . . .").

_____

_____

_____

6. How do you think the author intended to make the reader feel with this ending? Did you feel this way?

_____

_____

_____

_____

SAME OLD SONG?

The novel ends with the words to a song. It is similar to, but not the same as, the song that Stanley's family has sung for generations.

1. Who is singing this song? _____

2. To whom is this person singing? _____

3. Where do you think this person learned this song? Cite evidence from the novel to support your answer.

   _____

   _____

4. Compare and contrast this version of the song with the one that has been sung in Stanley's family for generations.

   a. Begin by writing the lyrics to each song:

Song from Stanley's Family	Song from Chapter 50

   b. What do these songs have in common? Think about the way they're sung, the feeling behind them, etc.

   _____

   _____

   _____

   c. Do you see any differences in the meanings of these two songs? And if so, what do you think these differences say about each family?

   _____

   _____

   _____

SECTION VI LOG-IN

Now that you have finished reading the novel, take some time to add to your Interactive Novel Log.

✦ **First, make a prediction about what will happen next in the lives of some of the novel's characters.**

Go further into the future than the author does in Chapter 50. Use your "Crystal Ball" worksheet (page 15) to do this.

✦ **Next, make a more personal connection to what you have read.**

Choose one of the suggestions below and use it to fill a page in your Interactive Novel Log. Take this opportunity to connect with the novel in a way that appeals to you.

✦ + ✦

Ideas for Your Interactive Novel Log

1
Drawing Diagrams

Zero draws a diagram in the dirt to help communicate his idea to Stanley. Using only shapes and arrows, draw your own diagram that shows how to get from one place on your school's campus to another place. At the bottom of your page, write about how easy or difficult you think it would be for someone to follow your diagram and understand what it is trying to communicate.

2
Another Palindrome

Zero's newly learned ability to read helped him solve the mystery of the suitcase's rightful owner. Zero asks Stanley if his name is spelled the same forwards and backwards. A word, name, or phrase that is spelled the same in either direction is called a palindrome. Come up with another character whose name is a palindrome. Give some information about this oddly named new character.

3
Selling Sploosh

You are in charge of marketing Sploosh to new customers. Create a magazine ad for Sploosh. You can come up with a snappy new slogan, feature any celebrity you choose, and design an eye-catching container for the product. Think about all the information you would want to know about such a product, and include those details in your advertisement.

4
Family Song

The novel ends with a familiar song that has unfamiliar words. Nearly the same song has been sung in different families for many generations. Do one of two things:

1. Make new lyrics to this song and explain what these new words mean to you.

2. Write the words to a song that is special to your family, and explain what this song means to you.

TEACHER INSTRUCTIONS

After your students have finished reading *Holes*, they can further their in-depth analysis of the novel through the use of the following worksheets:

+ +

Activity: "Add It Up"　　　　　　　**Page #:** 55–57　　　　　**Learning Type:** Individual
Description: Use the work done in the Interactive Novel Logs to sum up thoughts on the novel as a whole.

Activity: "A Better Letter?"　　　　　**Page #:** 58　　　　　　**Learning Type:** Individual
Description: Write a letter from Stanley to his mother. Tell her what really happens at Camp Green Lake.

Activity: "An Honest Ad?"　　　　　　**Page #:** 59　　　　　　**Learning Type:** Collaborative
Description: As a group, design a promotional product for Camp Green Lake. Consider audience, intent, focus, and format prior to creation.

Activity: "A New Point of View"　　　　**Page #:** 60　　　　　　**Learning Type:** Individual
Description: Rewrite a scene in the novel from a first-person perspective. Think about how point of view affects story.

Activity: "Considering Genre"　　　　　**Page #:** 61　　　　　　**Learning Type:** Individual
Description: Give reasons why the novel could fit into more than one genre. Rewrite a scene from the novel in an entirely different genre.

Activity: "Filling In the Holes"　　　　　**Page #:** 62–63　　　　　**Learning Type:** Individual
Description: Imagine the events that transpired during one of the novel's many missing time periods. Explain why you chose a particular scene and how you chose to write it.

Activity: "A Character Interview"　　　　**Page #:** 64–65　　　　　**Learning Type:** Collaborative
Description: In pairs, role-play as a character and an interviewer in front of the class. Utilize the tips provided on page 65.

Activity: "A Novel Poster"　　　　　　**Page #:** 66–67　　　　　**Learning Type:** Collaborative
Description: Collaborate to create a poster that identifies key points in a chapter and shows understanding of the elements that contribute to that chapter's success. (**TIP:** Follow the detailed teacher instructions provided on page 66.)

Activity: "Connect the Plots"　　　　　**Page #:** 68–69　　　　　**Learning Type:** Collaborative
Description: In front of the class, demonstrate connections between the people, places, and things that populate the novel. (**TIP:** Follow the detailed teacher instructions provided on page 68.)

Activity: "Family Fortune"　　　　　　**Page #:** 70–71　　　　　**Learning Type:** Individual
Description: Plan and write a persuasive essay about the luck (or lack thereof) of Stanley's family. Use the checklists on page 71 to stay focused and on task. (**TIP:** Assign partners to complete the peer-editing form on the bottom of page 71.)

Activity: "A Persuasive Letter"　　　　**Page #:** 72　　　　　　**Learning Type:** Individual
Description: Use a letter-writing format to construct an argument and support that opinion with evidence from the text.

Activity: "My Book Rating"　　　　　　**Page #:** 73　　　　　　**Learning Type:** Individual
Description: Rate different components of the story before making a final evaluation of the book as a whole.

NAME: _____

ADD IT UP

A novel is the sum of its parts. It is a combination of the events (plot) and people (characters) it describes. Look back at the work you have done as you have read each section of *Holes*. Decide how the parts add up to form the novel as a whole.

| What Happened When? |

Now that you have finished the novel — and have had a lot of practice with summarization — use your skills to write a very brief summary of the entire novel. Fit your statement on the lines below. In order to do so, include only the most important events in your summary.

_____

_____

_____

_____

_____

_____

_____

_____

_____

_____

Now your teacher will read you the Book Summary included in the teacher guide (page 7). Listen closely and answer the following questions.

1. Was there anything you felt this summary should have included but didn't?

_____

_____

2. Would this summary give someone who hasn't read the book a good idea of what to expect? Explain.

_____

_____

3. Would you say that this book is easy or challenging to summarize? Give reasons for your opinion.

_____

_____

NAME: _____

ADD IT UP (CONT.)

A Dynamic Protagonist

1. Look back at your answers to question #2 for each section. In which section did Stanley undergo the biggest, most permanent change?

   _____

2. Why do you think he changed so much at that point in the novel? Was there one big event or a series of small events that led to his transformation?

   _____

   _____

   _____

Major Minors

Choose two of the minor characters listed. Compare and contrast these two characters. Think about who they are as people and the roles they play in the events of the novel. Begin by checking the box next to each character.

❑ the Warden	❑ X-Ray	❑ Elya Yelnats
❑ Mr. Sir	❑ Zero	❑ Kate Barlow
❑ Mr. Pendanski	❑ Zigzag	❑ Trout Walker

1. How are these two characters similar? _____

   _____

   _____

2. How are these two characters different? _____

   _____

   _____

3. How would the novel have been different without these two characters? Which one is more important to the novel, in your opinion? Explain.

   _____

   _____

   _____

   _____

ADD IT UP (CONT.)

All Types of Trouble

Look back at your notes in your Interactive Novel Log. You wrote about three types of conflict. In your opinion, which one presented the most difficulty for Stanley throughout the course of the novel? Which one did he most need to overcome in order to become a happier, healthier person? Check the box next to your choice.

❑ **Person vs. Person** ❑ **Person vs. Self** ❑ **Person vs. Nature**

Explain your choice. Why would you say that overcoming this type of conflict was the most important to Stanley's story?

_____

_____

_____

_____

_____

_____

_____

_____

Crystal Ball

Look back at your predictions for each section of *Holes*.

1. Which of your predictions came true just like you thought they would?

_____

_____

_____

2. Which of your predictions were very different from what ended up happening in the novel?

_____

_____

_____

_____

NAME: _____

A BETTER LETTER?

While at Camp Green Lake, Stanley writes home to his mother, but he does not tell the truth about his experiences. What would a more truthful letter look like?

Choose one of Stanley's experiences from his time at Camp Green Lake. Write a letter to Stanley's mother as if you are Stanley. Tell her what is really happening. Then answer the question at the bottom of this page.

Dear Mom,

_____

_____

_____

_____

_____

_____

_____

_____

_____

_____

_____

_____

_____

+ +

What Do You Think?

Should Stanley have sent this type of letter to his mother? How might a truthful letter have been a better idea than what he wrote? How might it have been worse? Write your thoughts here.

_____

_____

_____

_____

An Honest Ad?

Teacher Instructions

With this activity, your students will be tasked with designing and creating an advertisement for Camp Green Lake.

1. Divide the class into groups of 3–5 students each.

2. Cut out, copy, and distribute the handout below. Read it aloud in class to ensure that students understand the assignment. Stress the importance of deciding on audience, intent, focus, and format at an early stage in the creation process.

3. Assist students with the creation of their formats (e.g., creating a tri-fold brochure, using digital tools to create a video clip, displaying actual promotional postcards).

4. Allow the necessary time for students to complete their advertisements. This activity will most likely require multiple days for planning, creation, and sharing.

5. After every group has completed its project, conduct a class display time. Have each group share the media it has created. Prompt other groups to guess the intended audience for each advertisement, as well as its focus. Also ask other groups to name the intent of the ad and how well it achieves that intent.

+ +

Student Instructions

Vacancies don't last long at Camp Green Lake. That is true for most of the book, but at some point in the early days, the camp must have needed to advertise. How else would they have gotten their name out and become such a popular option for the court system?

Imagine your group has been asked to create an advertisement for Camp Green Lake. Work together to create a promotional product that will achieve its goal. In order to do so, you will need to decide as a group on four things:

✦ **Audience** — Who is your ad geared toward? Who are you trying to convince that Camp Green Lake is a worthwhile facility? Is it geared toward judges and courts? Is it intended to convince parents whose children are being sent there? Is it meant to convince the children themselves that this camp will make them better and stronger?

✦ **Intent** — How will you market the camp? Will your ad honestly focus on the harsh realities of the camp? Will you use *euphemisms* (pronounced *yoof uh miz ums*), which is when one intentionally uses pleasant words to describe unpleasant things?

✦ **Focus** — Will your group focus on the location and climate of the camp? Will it highlight the staff (counselors, owner, etc.)? Will it focus on what students will do each day and how they can unwind after a hard day's work?

✦ **Format** — What will your ad look like? Consider one of the following or come up with an idea of your own: **brochure** (fold a paper in thirds, create a cover and several pages of content), **postcards** (create a series of three postcards, each containing an image and a slogan), or **video clip**.

NAME: _____

A NEW POINT OF VIEW

Holes is written in the **third-person point of view**. The narrator is not a character in the book, and pronouns such as "he" and "him" are used when writing about Stanley's experiences. This means that we the readers can experience more than what Stanley experiences. We can know what other people are thinking or what they're doing when Stanley is not around. When a novel is written in **first-person point of view**, the author uses pronouns such as "I" and "me."

Choose an important scene from the novel. Rewrite a few paragraphs from that scene. This time, however, use the first-person point of view to show what happens.

_____

_____

_____

_____

_____

_____

_____

_____

_____

_____

_____

_____

_____

+ +

1. How do you think the novel would have changed if the author had used the first-person point of view?

_____

_____

2. Why do you think the author chose to use third-person perspective in this novel?

_____

_____

3. What about the author's writing style or tone allowed us to understand Stanley's thoughts and feelings even though the book is written in third-person?

_____

_____

NAME: _____

CONSIDERING GENRE

In literature, the word *genre* refers to the category a novel fits into. Some examples of genres are historical fiction, science fiction, fantasy, and contemporary fiction. Books that fit into a certain genre usually share similar form, style, or subject matter.

Holes mostly takes place in the real world and contains people and settings that could be possible. This would put it in the genre of *realistic fiction*. However, the novel also has a few elements of magic in it, which could make it a part of the genre known as *magic realism*.

List elements of the story that seem very realistic: _____

_____

_____

List elements of the story that seem more magical: _____

_____

_____

Imagine if *Holes* had been written in a completely different genre. Choose and circle one of the genres below. Then rewrite a short scene from *Holes*, but change the action so that it best fits into this new genre. Use a separate piece of paper if more room is needed.

adventure	fable	fantasy	science fiction

_____

_____

_____

_____

_____

_____

_____

_____

_____

_____

_____

_____

_____

NAME: _____

FILLING IN THE HOLES

In several places in *Holes*, a character goes through a transformation or has an important experience that we do not get to read about. We never really know what happens during these experiences. Can you imagine what might have happened?

Choose one from the list below. Write the story that is not told in *Holes*. You may choose to write your story in the first-person perspective as if you were that character, or you may write in the voice of a third-person narrator.

A. the three days between when Sam is killed and when Miss Katherine becomes Kissin' Kate Barlow

B. the 17 days the first Stanley Yelnats spends lost in the desert near God's Thumb

C. the two years Trout Walker and Linda Miller get married, lose their money, and search for Miss Katherine

D. the days Zero spends in the desert after he hits Mr. Pendanski and before he hears Stanley walking up to his boat

E. the time at the camp between when Stanley crashes Mr. Sir's truck and when he and Zero return to dig for the treasure

F. the time between when Stanley and Zero leave Camp Green Lake and when the Warden is forced to sell the land to a well-intentioned organization

G. the year and a half between when Stanley and Zero left Camp Green Lake and when the final scene of the novel takes place

✦ ✦

Use the space below and on the next page to write your story.

_____

_____

_____

_____

_____

_____

_____

_____

_____

_____

NAME: _____

FILLING IN THE HOLES (CONT.)

Continue your story here, and then answer the questions below.

_____

_____

_____

_____

_____

_____

_____

_____

_____

_____

_____

_____

_____

_____

+ +

Considering Craft

1. Why did you choose this particular story to write about? Explain what made this storyline so interesting to you.

_____

_____

_____

2. In which perspective did you write your story, first-person or third-person?

_____

Explain why you chose this perspective.

_____

_____

_____

NAME(S): _____

A CHARACTER INTERVIEW

Stanley is the main character in *Holes*, but the other characters are important, too. The secondary characters help readers understand the main character better and help move the plot along. You and a partner will analyze one secondary character and create a mock interview that demonstrates the character's personality.

Your teacher will assign one of these secondary characters to you and your partner:

❑ the Warden   ❑ X-Ray   ❑ Zero

❑ Mr. Sir   ❑ Zigzag   ❑ Madame Zeroni

❑ Mr. Pendanski   ❑ Magnet   ❑ Miss Katherine/Kate Barlow

> **Once you have been assigned a character, write his or her name here:**
>
> _____

You and your partner will present a live interview of your assigned character. One of you will pretend to be the character, while the other will be the interviewer. Work together to plan your interview. Write five questions you would like to ask your assigned character. Use questions that require more than a one-word answer. In order to do this, use question starters such as the following:

1. Tell us about _____

   _____

2. What did you think when _____

   _____

3. How would you _____

   _____

4. Explain why _____

   _____

Now come up with a question of your own.

5. _____

   _____

NAME(S): _____

A Character Interview (CONT.)
Makings of a Great Interview

You and your partner will be conducting an interview in front of the class, so you both will want to make it great. First and foremost, you will want to be prepared.

✦ Discuss the types of questions the interviewer will be asking.

✦ Discuss how the character would answer these questions.

✦ Practice your presentation!

In addition, each member of the team can use a few helpful tips to make the interview a success.

Interviewer

❑ Before the actual presentation, prepare note cards with brief hints that will help you remember your opening statement, the questions you will be asking, etc.

❑ Begin by giving the audience a brief introduction to the character.

❑ Explain how the character knows Stanley (or knows one of his descendants).

❑ Provide an interesting fact about the character.

❑ Ask at least four questions. Remember to make your questions ones that require more than a one-word answer.

❑ Be sure to listen to the interviewee's responses and wait until your partner is finished speaking before moving on to the next question.

❑ Conclude the interview by asking the audience if they have any questions for the character.

Interviewee

❑ Pretend that you are the character throughout the interview.

❑ Answer the questions as you imagine the character would answer them.

❑ If possible, try to talk and act the way you imagine the character would.

❑ Listen to the interviewer carefully and wait until he or she is finished asking each question before responding.

A NOVEL POSTER
TEACHER INSTRUCTIONS

This activity offers students an opportunity to demonstrate understanding of the novel by creating visual representations of its parts.

Materials Required: poster board, markers

Optional Materials: scissors, glue, magazines, Internet access, sticky notes

✦ To begin, divide the class into groups of students. The ideal number in each group is 4, but smaller or larger groups will also be possible.

✦ Next, assign a chapter from the novel to each group. Choose from the chapters listed on the student page.

✦ Distribute the second page of this activity. Have students read the instructions for what to include on their posters.

✦ Give students plenty of time to plan and create their posters. If you wish, allow them to access magazines or the Internet in search of appropriate images to include.

✦ After groups have completed their posters, hang the posters around the room. Conduct a gallery walk.

Ideas for a Gallery Walk

Allow students to move around the room and examine each poster. Equip students with sticky notes. When they have questions regarding other groups' posters, they can write their questions on sticky notes and attach these notes directly to the posters. Use the following prompts to guide your students to ask questions about the posters:

✦ Is an idea on the poster not clear?

✦ Do you disagree with a point the poster makes?

✦ Do you want more information about something the group has included?

✦ Do you want to ask how the group felt about any particular scene or character?

✦ Do you want to bring up something you thought was important in that chapter but isn't included on the poster?

Once students have completed this process, allow groups to answer the questions attached to their posters.

A NOVEL POSTER (CONT.)

Your group will work together to create a poster that represents one chapter from *Holes*. Your teacher will assign your group one of the following chapters.

Chapter 3	**Chapter 13**	**Chapter 32**
Chapter 7 (Stanley)	**Chapter 18**	**Chapter 38**
Chapter 7 (Elya)	**Chapter 25**	**Chapter 44**
Chapter 9	**Chapter 30**	**Chapter 47**

Our group has been assigned Chapter _____.

First, your group should discuss the events in your chapter and decide which details are the most important.

Your poster should contain the following elements. Write who will be in charge of each.

#	Elements	Assigned to
1	• the number of the chapter • a short explanation of what happens in this chapter	
2	• a quotation from this chapter • a short explanation of the significance of the quotation	
3	• a picture representing the most important event in this chapter • a short description of the event	
4	• a picture that represents the setting of this event • a one-sentence explanation of where the event takes place	

Tips for Making Posters

✦ **Be creative!** You may draw pictures, use pictures from magazines, print images from the Internet (with permission from your teacher), or paste on objects that relate to the story.

✦ **Plan before you start.** Everyone should collect pictures and ideas before anyone begins writing on the poster board. Work together to design the look of the poster by placing all pictures before you paste them. Don't forget to leave room for the written parts.

CONNECT THE PLOTS
TEACHER INSTRUCTIONS

One of the major themes of *Holes* is how everything is connected. Events from the past are connected to the present, and people who seem to be strangers turn out to have affected Stanley and his family in significant ways. Even everyday objects like onions and old shoes have a way of being important and showing up in multiple times and places. Use this "Six Degrees of Separation"-style activity to illustrate the connectedness of the people, places, and things in *Holes*.

1. **Create a bulletin board of labels.** You may choose to do this in a variety of ways. Labels are provided for you on the following page. You may use pushpins to attach these labels on a bulletin board, or you can affix magnets to the backs of the labels and place them on a whiteboard. A third option would be to write the labels on a chalkboard. In all instances, the labels should be placed in a random order on the board.

2. **Randomly announce two people, places, and/or things from the labels.** Place a second set of labels in a hat or other container. Pull out two labels and read each aloud. Some combinations of people, places, and things will have obvious connections. Others will require a few intermediate connections to be made first.

3. **Explain to students how they will be illustrating the connection between these two people, places, and/or things.** If using pushpins on a bulletin board, give students string or yarn. Have them hook the yarn onto the pushpin affixed to the first label. Then have them pull the yarn over to the next label if there is a direct connection. If there is not, students must pull the yarn to a direct connection and continue to do this until they make a connection with the second label chosen by you. If a whiteboard/chalkboard is used, follow the same logic as detailed above by having students use whiteboard pens/chalk to draw lines between the connections.

4. **Choose a student to illustrate the connection between these two people, places, and/or things.** Allow students to demonstrate speaking skills as they explain these connections. For most combinations of objects, students will need to make intermediate connections in order to connect the two original items. As a student makes each connection, he or she will explain the connection aloud to the class. For example, if the two labels chosen are "Myra Menke" and "Onions," a student might say the following as he or she is demonstrating the connection at the board:

    "Myra Menke" was the love interest of "Elya Yelnats," who was the father of "Stanley Yelnats I," who survived for 17 days in the mountains near "God's Thumb," which is where "Onions" have grown for over a century.

5. **Allow discussion.** Give students an opportunity to agree or disagree with the speaker. Also allow them to offer other ways of connecting the two people, places, or things.

6. **Repeat this process until each student has had a chance to go to the board.**

CONNECT THE PLOTS (CONT.)
LABELS

Note: There are two Mary Lou labels given below. Remind students that the names of aircraft, watercraft, etc., are *italicized* (as are the titles of books, movies, plays, etc.).

Stanley Yelnats IV	Stanley Yelnats III	Stanley Yelnats I
Elya Yelnats	Myra Menke	Madame Zeroni
Sarah Miller	Linda Miller	Trout Walker
Katherine Barlow	Sam	Zero
Barf Bag	Twitch	the Warden
Mr. Sir	Mr. Pendanski	Ms. Morengo
God's Thumb	Yellow-spotted Lizards	onions
spiced peaches	Clyde Livingston	foot fungus
Sploosh	Mary Lou (the donkey)	*Mary Lou* (the boat)

FAMILY FORTUNE
OUTLINE

For almost the entire novel, Stanley believes that he and his family have rotten luck. Yet, by the end of *Holes*, Stanley and his family are in a very different place from where they began. So where do you stand on Stanley's ideas about his family and their fortune (or lack thereof)? Were all of their previous struggles proof of their awful luck, or were they just the necessary steps that ultimately led to their happiness?

Your assignment is to write an essay in which you choose a side and attempt to persuade your reader that your position is the correct one. You must first communicate which side you have chosen, and then you must give examples from the text to support your choice.

+ +

Follow this outline in writing your essay. Use the space provided to brainstorm ideas and to plan your rough draft.

First, set up your essay by introducing the concept. State what your essay will be about and what your opinion is about this concept.

_____

_____

_____

_____

Next, state specific struggles that Stanley and/or his family has faced. Give examples from the book. Include quotations where appropriate.

Examples: _____

_____

_____

Quotations: _____

_____

Show how these struggles ultimately support your opinion. Give examples from the book. Include quotations where appropriate.

Examples: _____

_____

_____

Quotations: _____

_____

FAMILY FORTUNE (CONT.)

SELF-EDITING CHECKLIST

After writing your rough draft, use this checklist to make sure your essay has everything that is required. Check off the box next to each item once you have included that element in your essay.

- ☐ I have introduced the concept of luck and how it applies to Stanley's family.
- ☐ I have clearly stated my opinion of whether their luck was ultimately good or bad.
- ☐ I have given examples of struggles the family has faced.
- ☐ I have shown how the results of these examples support my opinion.
- ☐ I have included quotations from the novel to support my claims.
- ☐ Throughout my essay, I have used transition words to move from one example or paragraph to the next.
- ☐ I have checked my essay for spelling, punctuation, and grammar mistakes.

One thing I like about my essay is	One thing I need help with is

PEER-EDITING CHECKLIST

Have your partner read your essay, check a box for each statement, and respond to the questions below.

Reader's Name: _____ **Yes** **No**

- The purpose of the essay was clearly stated and introduced. ☐ ☐
- An opinion about the concept was clearly stated. ☐ ☐
- Several examples and results of the family's struggles were given. ☐ ☐
- Evidence (quotations) from the novel were used to support claims. ☐ ☐
- There are no spelling or grammar errors. ☐ ☐

Did the writer give good examples that supported his or her claim? Explain.

_____
_____
_____

NAME: _____

A PERSUASIVE LETTER

Imagine that another school is considering using *Holes* in its classrooms. First, they want your thoughts on the novel.

Write a letter to the principal of this imaginary school. Give your opinion of the book and explain why it should be taught there or why it should not.

Follow this outline, and then write your letter on a separate piece of paper.

Dear Principal,

Paragraph 1 should include this information:

➤ *the title of the book*
➤ *why and when you read this book*
➤ *your opinion of the book*
➤ *if other classes should read this book*

Paragraph 1 goes here.

Paragraph 2 should include this information:

➤ *one thing you liked or did not like about the book and why*
➤ *an example from the book*

Paragraph 2 goes here.

Paragraph 3 should include this information:

➤ *a second thing you liked or did not like about the book and why*
➤ *an example from the book*

Paragraph 3 goes here.

Concluding Sentence:

➤ *one sentence saying what you think the school should do*

Conclusion goes here.

Sincerely,

sign name ⟶ *Your signature*

print name ⟶ **Your name**

NAME: _____

MY BOOK RATING

What did you like or dislike about the book? Think about the story elements and rank each one. Use the following rating scale.

0 stars	1 star	2 stars	3 stars	4 stars	5 stars
☆☆☆☆☆	★☆☆☆☆	★★☆☆☆	★★★☆☆	★★★★☆	★★★★★
terrible	bad	okay	good	great	amazing!

Characters ☆☆☆☆☆

Reason: _____

Setting ☆☆☆☆☆

Reason: _____

Point of View ☆☆☆☆☆

Reason: _____

Plot ☆☆☆☆☆

Reason: _____

The Ending ☆☆☆☆☆

Reason: _____

Theme ☆☆☆☆☆

Reason: _____

Overall, I give this book _____ stars because _____

_____

_____

TEACHER INSTRUCTIONS

Holes contains vocabulary that is integral to the novel's setting and themes. Sachar chooses to use many words that reflect the circumstances and landscapes in which the characters find themselves.

On page 75 is a list of the most challenging and important vocabulary words found in *Holes*. These words are listed in the order in which they appear in the novel. The chapter in which the word can be found is listed in parentheses after each word.

Select words from these section lists to assign for the "Choice Words" Interactive Novel Log entries (see page 14).

Other Ideas for Assigning Vocabulary

✦ **Traditional Vocabulary Lesson** — Select a total of 10 to 20 words for the entire class to study and learn.

✦ **Personalized Vocabulary** — Post the lists in the classroom and allow students to select their own word or words to study.

✦ **Students as Teachers** — For each section, assign a different word to pairs or groups of students and have them do short presentations on the word's meaning and use.

After your students have finished reading the entire novel, review vocabulary from each section by using one or more of the following activities:

✦ **Create a crossword puzzle.** Use one vocabulary word from each section.

✦ **Write a poem.** Use one vocabulary word from each section.

✦ **Play a Jeopardy-style game.** Make a game board with definitions of the vocabulary words. Students or student groups compete to identify the correct words.

> This adverb means "skillfully" or "nimbly."

> What is **deftly**?

✦ **Hold a vocabulary-in-context contest!** Have students write short stories that properly use as many vocabulary words as they can. Select a few stories with the highest number of vocabulary words used, read them aloud to the class, and have the class vote for the story that made the best use of vocabulary words.

NOVEL VOCABULARY

For each word, the chapter number is given in parentheses. The words can be found in the novel in the order in which they are shown here.

Section I	Section II	Section III
shriveled (1)	predatory (8)	condemned (20)
stifling (3)	evaporated (9)	shrill (20)
descendants (3)	intensity (9)	recede (20)
gruff (3)	fossilized (10)	desolate (21)
perseverance (3)	compound (12)	coiled (21)
neglected (3)	glisten (13)	defiance (22)
violation (4)	engraved (13)	writhing (22)
wearily (5)	excavated (15)	astonishment (22)
scarcity (6)	intently (15)	afflict (23)
auctioned (6)	presumably (16)	concoctions (25)
vacancies (6)	character (18)	quivering (25)
defective (7)	penetrating (18)	urged (26)
compacted (7)	unearthed (19)	sparingly (27)
preposterous (7)	appreciate (19)	rummaging (28)
summoned (7)		
expanse (7)		

Section IV	Section V	Section VI
unbearably (29)	revving (33)	inexplicable (43)
barren (29)	refuge (33)	abruptly (43)
briefly (29)	systematic (33)	indistinct (43)
stranded (29)	shimmering (34)	cradled (43)
depriving (30)	mirage (34)	adjacent (43)
feeble (30)	grimly (34)	pronounced (44)
unconscious (30)	ventilation (35)	commotion (45)
constant (31)	defy (36)	illuminated (45)
fidgeting (32)	increments (37)	suppress (45)
deftly (32)	swarm (37)	initiate (46)
accelerated (32)	wrenching (37)	delirious (46)
	precipice (38)	etched (46)
	lapped (39)	rigid (46)
	deserted (40)	strenuous (46)
	indentation (40)	legitimate (47)
	contaminate (41)	detainees (40)
	fugitive (42)	indefinitely (48)
		neutralizes (50)

ANSWER KEY

For many of the questions in this resource, answers will vary and will be subject to interpretation. Accept student work that responds appropriately to the questions asked and provides evidence from the text when called for. Refer to the answers listed below when more specific responses may be needed.

+ +

Setting the Mood (page 18)

1. The setting of Camp Green Lake is first introduced.

Then and Now (page 20)
In the Present
Characters: Stanley, Magnet, Zero, Mr. Pendanski, Zigzag
Actions that Occur: Stanley starts to dig his first hole. It is very difficult. All of the other boys dig faster than he does. It takes him all day. He gets painful blisters on his hands. He puts the pile of dirt too close to his hole, so he has to spend time relocating it. He finally finishes and spits in his hole, just like the other boys do.

In the Past
Characters: Elya Yelnats, Myra Menke, Madame Zeroni, Myra's father, Igor

Actions that Occur: Elya is in love with Myra. He asks for her hand in marriage, but her father wants a pig in return. An older man named Igor offers a pig for Myra's hand. Elya tells Madame Zeroni about this. Though she thinks he should forget about Myra, she promises to help. She gives him a tiny pig and tells him to carry it to the top of a mountain each day and let it drink. The pig will get bigger, and he will get stronger. He promises that when the time comes, he will also carry Madame Zeroni up the mountain to drink. Elya and Igor's pigs are the same size. Myra doesn't know who to choose. Elya realizes she is not smart and doesn't love him. He leaves her to Igor, and he sets sail for America. He forgets to uphold his promise to Madame Zeroni.

The Boys of Group D (pages 24–25)

1.

Order	Nickname	Real Name
1	X-Ray	Rex
2	Armpit	Theodore
3	Squid	*not given*
4	Zigzag	Ricky
5	Magnet	José
6	Zero	*not given*
7	Caveman	Stanley

2. X-Ray is the leader of the group.

3. He finds out that the group has given him a nickname ("Caveman").

4. Accept appropriate responses.

5. X-Ray asks Stanley to give him anything interesting he finds. X-Ray says that he should benefit from any discovery because he has been there the longest and dug the most holes already.

6. X-ray gets the rest of the day off. The Warden shows interest in the boys' activities, and she has them dig many holes near where X-Ray had been digging.

7–8. Accept appropriate responses.

Chains of Events (page 29)

Mr. Sir storyline: Mr. Sir takes Stanley to the Warden. The Warden scratches Mr. Sir with the venomous nail polish, causing him great pain. Mr. Sir gets back at Stanley by refusing to fill his canteen. Mr. Pendanski gives Stanley extra water each time he drives the water truck.

Zero storyline: Zero digs part of Stanley's hole. Stanley agrees to teach Zero to read. Zero agrees to dig part of Stanley's hole each day in exchange for lessons. The other boys resent Stanley for resting while Zero digs part of his hole.

What It Really Means (page 31)

Chapter 20 last line: "He's not going to die," the Warden said. "Unfortunately for you."

What just happened: The Warden has just scratched Mr. Sir with the rattlesnake venom for bothering her about the sunflower seeds being stolen.

Implication: Mr. Sir is going to blame Stanley for the pain he is suffering, and he will do something to make life difficult for Stanley.

Chapter 21 last line: Zero's hole was smaller than the others.

What just happened: Stanley returns from the Warden's office and notices that his hole is almost completely finished.

Implication: Zero dug Stanley's hole for him.

The Onion Man (page 32)

1. Chapter 25
2. He pulls a cart and sells onions to people.

The Antagonists (page 33)

1. Miss Katherine (aka Kissin' Kate Barlow)
2. Accept appropriate responses. Students will most likely choose Trout Walker, Hattie Parker, and the sheriff.
3. His job is to protect the people of the town, but he refused to protect Sam. Instead, he tried to force her to kiss him in order to spare Sam's life.
4. Once she is bitten by the lizard, she also knows that there is nothing they can do to get her to tell Trout and his wife the location of the treasure. She knows that they will probably never find it.
5. The author dislikes Trout for being rude, cruel, and unintelligent.

All Kinds of Unkind (pages 36–37)

1. Zero
2. Zero
3. Mr. Pendanski calls all of the other campers by the names their parents gave them. Zero is the only one he calls by his nickname.
4. Accept appropriate responses.
5. He hit Stanley in the head with a shovel earlier.
7. They believed that people of different races should not kiss.
8. Accept appropriate responses. Students will most likely say that Trout was used to getting what he wanted, and he was rejected by Miss Katherine. Trout would have been furious to hear that she kissed a man who he felt was not his equal.

9–10. Accept appropriate responses.

The New Kid (page 38)

Real Name: Brian
Nickname: Twitch
Crime(s): stealing cars
Before: By talking about how he gets twitchy when he's around cars and how it just makes him want to steal them, Twitch puts the idea of stealing a car into Stanley's head.
During: When Stanley gets into Mr. Sir's truck, he can't figure out how to make it move. Twitch yells out that he should put it into gear, which makes the car move away from Mr. Sir and the other campers.

Left in Suspense (page 39)

1. *Give Him Hope:* His great-grandfather survived for 17 days at a place called God's Thumb, and Stanley thinks he sees this place in the distance. There must be water or something there to sustain life.

   Make Him Feel Hopeless: Stanley has no water, he doesn't know if Zero is still alive, the desert is hot and dry.
2. his canteen
3. empty, empty, empty

Desert Decisions (page 42)

1. He realizes that he can only walk halfway as far as he's able to walk. If he walks as far as he can possibly walk, then he won't have the strength to walk back to the camp.
2. The holes are dug out in random locations. He is able to see the hills more clearly. There is an overturned boat lying in the desert.
3. He thinks they will not survive much longer without water. He can see that Zero is in bad shape and needs medical attention.
4. He is certain that he has dug his last hole. He will not go back to the place where he is forced to dig holes and take the abuse of Mr. Pendanski and the other counselors.
6. He decides to go look for the treasure near where he found the gold tube. He feels that the only way he and Zero can have the means to survive as outlaws is to find the treasure.

A Tale of Two (page 44)

2. Stanley helps Zero by carrying him up the mountain, giving him water, feeding him onions, etc. Zero helps Stanley by giving him Sploosh, lifting him up the rock with the shovel, and by telling him that he knows Stanley didn't steal the shoes.
3. Students will most likely say that Stanley is better equipped at this point. This is surprising since Zero had been used to living on his own out in the world, and Stanley has been overweight and lacking in confidence.
4. In this scene, we see that Sam and his onions helped the people of Green Lake tremendously. In fact, his onions may have saved the life of a child who had eaten bad meat.

ANSWER KEY (CONT.)

A Change in Stanley (page 45)

1. He is happier than he can remember being in a long time.

2. He thinks he might be near death and having delusions.

4. His plan is to slip back into camp and, while everyone is sleeping, dig for the treasure in the hole where he found the tube. He also plans to fill up on water and steal some food from the camp.

5. He is excited by the thought that this could be his destiny and that he likes the new him who is capable of doing such things. He is troubled by the idea that it will be difficult to contact his family and he may never see them again.

The Return to Camp (page 48)

1. They are hoping to find the treasure and also get some food and water.

2. They are bonding and becoming good friends. Zero talks a lot more than he usually does. He shares with Stanley stories of his childhood. The two also play a game where they try to get the other to drink water first.

3.

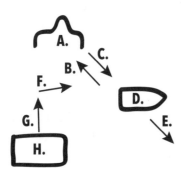

A. God's Thumb

B. They walked straight toward the peak.

C. They traveled back from the peak.

D. *Mary Lou* (the boat)

E. They are walking away from camp.

F. They turned right toward boat.

G. They walked away from camp.

H. Camp Green Lake

4. The other drawing was of the engraved design on the tube Stanley found. Accept appropriate responses to the second part of the question.

5. They hear the sounds of voices. They see a cluster of holes.

While They Were Gone (page 49)

Group D: They lifted the truck out of the hole.

The case: Stanley's innocence was proven because it was discovered that he was in the school bathroom being bullied at the time the shoes were stolen.

The files: They disappeared. Mr. Pendanski followed the Warden's orders to destroy them.

Stanley's family: His father invented a product that eliminates foot odor.

Layer by Layer (page 50)

1. Sam

2. Accept appropriate responses. Students may say that Sam and the onions both represent wholesomeness and/or naturalness. They are both good and helpful.

3. Onions have many layers. This novel has many layers in its plot and with its characters. Those layers all work together to form the whole novel.

The Final Chapter (page 51)

1. The Warden was forced to sell it to an organization for girls. It is set to become a Girl Scout camp.

2. Mr. Sir was fond of saying, "This isn't a Girl Scout camp." Soon, it actually will be.

3. jewels of low quality, stocks and other papers worth a lot of money

4. The descendant of Elya Yelnats finally carried a descendant of Madame Zeroni up the mountain to sing the song and drink the water.

5. Zero has been reunited with his mother. They seem to be happy and comfortable together. She sings him the song that has been in their family since at least the time of Madame Zeroni.

Same Old Song? (page 52)

1. Zero's mother

2. Zero

3. She learned this song from her family. We know it has been in her family since at least the time of Madame Zeroni, who taught the song to Elya Yelnats.

4. a. Students should copy each version of the song. The song from Stanley's family can be found at the end of Chapter 39.

   b. Accept appropriate responses. Students may say that both songs are melancholy (sad), both are sung about animal characters, and both are sung to the same melody.

MEETING STANDARDS

The lessons and activities included in *Rigorous Reading: An In-Depth Guide to Holes* meet the following Common Core State Standards for grades 5–8. (©Copyright 2010. National Governors Association Center for Best Practices and Council of Chief State School Officers. All right reserved.)

The code for each standard covered in this resource is listed in the table below and on page 80. The codes are listed in boldface, and the page numbers of the activities that meet that standard are listed in regular type. For more information about the Common Core State Standards and for a full listing of the descriptions associated with each code, go to *http://www.corestandards.org/* or visit *http://www.teachercreated.com/standards/*.

Here is an example of an English Language Arts (ELA) code and how to read it:

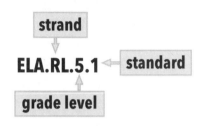

ELA Strands

L = Language
W = Writing
RL = Reading: Literature
SL = Speaking and Listening

+ +

Strand Reading: Literature   **Substrand** Key Ideas and Details

ELA.RL.5.1, ELA.RL.6.1, ELA.RL.7.1, ELA.RL.8.1: 11, 13–14, 16–18, 20, 22–25, 28, 31, 33, 35–39, 41–42, 44–45, 47–49, 51–52, 70–71

ELA.RL.5.2, ELA.RL.6.2, ELA.RL.7.2, ELA.RL.8.2: 10–13, 16, 18, 20, 22, 24–25, 28–31, 33, 35–39, 41–45, 47–49, 51, 55–57, 70–71

ELA.RL.5.3: 10, 12–13, 16, 20, 22, 24–25, 28–33, 35–39, 41–44, 47–52, 56–57, 68–71

ELA.RL.6.3: 10–13, 16, 18, 20, 22–25, 28–33, 35–39, 41–45, 47–52, 55–57, 68–71

ELA.RL.7.3: 10–13, 16–20, 22–25, 28–33, 35–39, 41–45, 47–52, 55–57, 68–71

ELA.RL.8.3: 10–13, 16, 18, 20, 22–26, 28–33, 35–39, 41–45, 47–52, 55–58, 68–71

Strand Reading: Literature   **Substrand** Craft and Structure

ELA.RL.5.4, ELA.RL.6.4, ELA.RL.7.4, ELA.RL.8.4: 13–14, 16–20, 22–26, 28, 30–33, 35–37, 39, 41–42, 44–45, 47–48, 50–52, 58, 60, 74–75

ELA.RL.5.5, ELA.RL.6.5, ELA.RL.7.5: 17–18, 20, 23–25, 29–33, 36–39, 42–45, 48–52, 55–58, 62–63, 68–71

ELA.RL.5.6: 17, 19–20, 23, 26, 30–31, 33, 36–37, 39, 42–45, 48–52, 58, 60, 62–65, 70–71

ELA.RL.6.6: 11, 16–20, 22–26, 28, 31, 33, 35–37, 39, 41–42, 44–45, 47–52, 56–58, 60, 62–63, 70–71

ELA.RL.7.6: 12, 16, 22, 24–26, 28, 30, 32–33, 35–39, 41–42, 44–45, 47–52, 56–57, 60, 62–65

ELA.RL.8.6: 19, 24–26, 33, 36–37, 44–45, 49–52, 58, 60, 62–65

Strand Reading: Literature   **Substrand** Integration of Knowledge and Ideas

ELA.RL.5.7: 48

Strand Reading: Literature   **Substrand** Range of Reading and Level of Text Complexity

ELA.RL.5.10, ELA.RL.6.10, ELA.RL.7.10, ELA.RL.8.10: 10–75

MEETING STANDARDS (CONT.)

+ +

Strand Writing　　　　　　　**Substrand** Text Types and Purposes

ELA.W.5.1, ELA.W.6.1, ELA.W.7.1, ELA.W.8.1: 15–18, 20, 22–26, 28, 30–33, 35–37, 39, 41–42, 44, 47–48, 50–52, 55–58, 60, 63, 70–72

ELA.W.5.2, ELA.W.6.2, ELA.W.7.2, ELA.W.8.2: 10, 12–14, 16–18, 20, 22–25, 28–29, 31–33, 35–39, 41–45, 47–52, 55–58, 60–61, 63, 70–72

ELA.W.5.3, ELA.W.6.3, ELA.W.7.3, ELA.W.8.3: 26, 38, 58, 60–63

Strand Writing　　　　　　　**Substrand** Production and Distribution of Writing

ELA.W.5.4, ELA.W.6.4, ELA.W.7.4, ELA.W.8.4: 10, 16, 21–23, 26–29, 34–35, 40–41, 46–47, 49, 53, 55, 57–63, 70–72

ELA.W.5.5, ELA.W.6.5, ELA.W.7.5, ELA.W.8.5: 59, 70–72

Strand Writing　　　　　　　**Substrand** Research to Build and Present Knowledge

ELA.W.5.9, ELA.W.6.9, ELA.W.7.9, ELA.W.8.9: 10–75

Strand Writing　　　　　　　**Substrand** Range of Writing

ELA.W.5.10, ELA.W.6.10, ELA.W.7.10, ELA.W.8.10: 8–73

+ +

Strand Speaking and Listening　　　**Substrand** Comprehension and Collaboration

ELA.SL.5.1, ELA.SL.6.1, ELA.SL.7.1, ELA.SL.8.1: 19, 23, 30, 43, 50, 59, 64–69

ELA.SL.5.2, ELA.SL.6.2, ELA.SL.7.2, ELA.SL.8.2: 19, 30

ELA.SL.5.3, ELA.SL.6.3, ELA.SL.7.3, ELA.SL.8.3: 30, 43

Strand Speaking and Listening　　　**Substrand** Presentation of Knowledge and Ideas

ELA.SL.5.4, ELA.SL.6.4, ELA.SL.7.4, ELA.SL.8.4: 64–69

ELA.SL.5.5, ELA.SL.6.5, ELA.SL.7.5, ELA.SL.8.5: 66–69

ELA.SL.5.6, ELA.SL.6.6, ELA.SL.7.6, ELA.SL.8.6: 64–65

+ +

Strand Language　　　　　　**Substrand** Conventions of Standard English

ELA.L.5.1, ELA.L.6.1, ELA.L.7.1, ELA.L.8.1: 8–73

ELA.L.5.2, ELA.L.6.2, ELA.L.7.2, ELA.L.8.2: 8–73

Strand Language　　　　　　**Substrand** Knowledge of Language

ELA.L.5.3, ELA.L.6.3, ELA.L.7.3, ELA.L.8.3: 8–75

Strand Language　　　　　　**Substrand** Vocabulary Acquisition and Use

ELA.L.5.4, ELA.L.6.4, ELA.L.7.4, ELA.L.8.4: 8–75

ELA.L.5.5, ELA.L.6.5, ELA.L.7.5, ELA.L.8.5: 8–75

ELA.L.5.6, ELA.L.6.6, ELA.L.7.6, ELA.L.8.6: 8–75